A SOLUTION TO WEALTH INEQUALITY

CHRIS KELLY

ISBN-13: 979-8-9882633-3-3 (Paperback edition)

ISBN-13: 979-8-9882633-5-7 (Hardback edition)

ISBN-13: 979-8-9882633-4-0 (eBook edition)

For my sons.

It is not the man who has too little, but the man who craves more, that is poor.

— SENECA

CONTENTS

Preface 1
1. What is wealth and why do we hoard it? 11
2. The Wealth Gap 19
3. How money actually works 30
4. What's your Number? 39
5. The problems generosity could solve 50
6. How not to solve this problem 68
7. The case for persuasion 79
8. Persuasion by altruism (and pure logic) 84
9. Persuasion by fear 94
10. Persuasion by redirection 99
11. Why persuasion works better than force 107
12. Rethinking wealth and generosity 112

Acknowledgements 121
Appendix A: Referenced Materials 123
Appendix B: My Number 131
Appendix C: $270 billion per year for housing 137
About the Author 141

PREFACE

"We've heard enough about Bliz-blaz and Him-ham already. Get to the bloody point!"
— C. Montgomery Burns

This is a work of rhetoric. Or maybe it's a manifesto. It's not a thoroughly researched treatise. There are no appeals to academic authority, no quotes from experts, no claims of expertise at all in fact. I'm not an expert on wealth inequality and don't pretend to be. I have no credentials.

My only qualification to write this book is that I'm a wealthy person concerned about inequality, and I have a perspective on it that I feel needs to be shared. For years, I've watched with glazed eyes as politicians, pundits, and academics make the same tired points, which the wealthy have long since tuned out. I've wondered how so many wealthy people continue to pursue a perilous and unsatisfying path, and why obvious arguments for change remain unmade. I've marveled at how completely everyone talks past each other.

There's a more productive conversation we could be having, and this book is my attempt to start it. I'm not here to summarize the latest research or opine on other people's arguments and ideas. The ideas here are mine, and because I only have so many of them—and because I'd rather you finish and share a short book than abandon a long one—I promise to get to the bloody point as succinctly as possible. If you get to the end and think I've left something out, I'm happy to continue the conversation online.[1]

This preface summarizes my main arguments and the rest of the book fills in the details. Here it is in three bullets:

- Wealth inequality is breaking society, and politicians are not coming to the rescue.
- The wealthy must be persuaded to change their behavior, force will not work.
- Solving this problem requires a shift in our cultural attitudes toward wealth and generosity.

This book provides real solutions and specific actions we can all take to address inequality. Let's begin.

Wealth inequality is a real problem

When I was a kid in the mid-1990s, Bill Gates became the first person in history to have a net worth exceeding $10 billion; today, there are hundreds of billionaires you've never heard of worth more than this, and more than 3,000 billionaires worldwide.[2] When I was a kid, it was safe to assume the average person I knew would make more money and live longer than their parents; today, for the first time

1. Here's where you can find me.
Reddit: reddit.com/r/wealthinequality
Substack: wealthinequality.substack.com
Website: abovewealth.org

2. There is also one trillionaire, Elon Musk, with a net worth equivalent to more than 3% of the GDP of the United States, surpassing the previous record held by John D. Rockefeller.

since World War II, that's no longer true. When I was a kid, we had a balanced federal budget; today, we've racked up trillions in debt trying to stimulate an economy where the average American can no longer afford to buy a home.

There are a lot of people who will try to explain all of this away and claim inequality isn't actually a problem. They'll say inequality has always existed. They'll say it simply reflects differences in talent, work ethic, and value creation. They'll say there's no way to intervene without breaking capitalism. While some of these arguments have merit up to a point, none stand up to real scrutiny. With few exceptions, those denying this problem are advocating for their own ability to accumulate wealth, or they work for a wealthy person, or they expect to be wealthy themselves someday and don't want to rock the boat. Few will try to argue in good faith that wealth inequality poses no problem for society.

With that said, some readers of this book are already convinced inequality is a problem, and some are not. The latter group might want to see the point proven, but for the former—which I can safely assume is the vast majority of readers—I'd just be preaching to the converted.[3] Therefore, rather than thickening this book with points others have already made quite compellingly, I'll direct the doubters to check out "Further Reading on the Topic of Inequality" in Appendix A. There, you will find a range of reputable publications all making the case for why inequality is a serious and growing problem.

If you've followed this topic, you're probably familiar with statistics in the vein of "The top X% of people in Y place control Z% of the wealth." You won't find much of that here, as such factoids are just different ways of saying inequality is a problem. This book is primarily concerned with solutions and treats the existence of the problem as so obvious it barely needs elaboration.

---

3. A recent YouGov poll found that 80% of Americans think the gap between rich and poor is either a "very big" or "somewhat big" problem.

https://yougov.com/en-us/articles/53821-majorities-americans-say-wealth-inequality-is-problem-want-government-intervention-january-2-5-2026-economist-yougov-poll

Our instincts haven't caught up to modern reality

I'm old enough to remember when the internet was relegated to a beige box that tied up the landline when I went on AOL. Today, the internet permeates everything and has created fortunes that were unimaginable just a generation ago. It has transformed the economy and society so quickly that our cultural norms, which come from millions of years of evolution and thousands of years of history, simply haven't caught up.

Biology doesn't know who the billionaires are. It screams at all of us to hoard resources, even those with more than they could spend in a thousand lifetimes. Because we're all running this software, and because rich people have always maximized their wealth, we don't question the practice. That doesn't mean we all love billionaires and think what they're doing is great—it just means we don't expect them to act any differently than they have.

We're also ill-equipped to grapple with the size of their fortunes. Speaking for myself, I had no idea of the compounding nature of wealth until I made my first million dollars in my late twenties. I was raised by parents who had to work every day just to pay the bills, so it was a revelation to me how much money I could make off money itself. But this is precisely how the rich get richer. Eventually, net worth reaches a level where it becomes impossible to spend the returns it generates, let alone the principal. For those who need to constantly earn money to stay ahead of their expenses, it's natural to assume the ultra wealthy are doing the same thing at a different scale. It's harder to grasp how unspendable their fortunes really are, and therefore how unnecessary their continued accumulation is.

In the face of rising inequality, it's no surprise we've looked to what appears to be the best tool we have to fight the problem: taxes. However, despite decades of effort by politicians and activists, the tax code remains broken and the wealth gap keeps growing. While it's true that better tax policy can and should play a role in reducing inequality, this tax-first approach is doomed to fail for a variety of reasons that I'll explore in greater depth later in the book. For now, I'll just share one thought.

Let's imagine that by some miracle, Congress manages to push through a tax bill that's exactly what Bernie Sanders and Elizabeth Warren want: highly progressive income tax rates, a wealth tax, capital gains taxed as ordinary income, closed loopholes—the full progressive wish list. We might consider this a victory, but without persuasion it will be fleeting. If the wealthy feel they've been defeated by force, they'll lobby aggressively to repeal these reforms, do whatever they can to evade taxes, and potentially feel aggrieved to the point that they pull back on philanthropy. By contrast, if we can persuade wealthy people that giving up their excess billions is in everyone's best interest, including theirs, they will do so voluntarily. We will not have to worry about them fighting us because we will have brought them on side. Instead of an enemy we have to constantly keep in check—like Russia after the Cold War or the Taliban in Afghanistan—we will have created powerful new allies, like Germany and Japan after World War II.

The challenge, of course, is to effect this change in mindset among the ultra wealthy. So how do we do that?

We have to make them want to solve the problem

In his seminal work, *How to Win Friends and Influence People*, Dale Carnegie had this to say about persuasion: "There is only one way under high heaven to get anybody to do anything. Did you ever stop to think of that? Yes, just one way. And that is by making the other person want to do it." If you take one idea away from this entire book, it's this. The key to solving wealth inequality is getting rich people to *want* to solve it.

To do this, we first need to spread the idea that every wealthy person should determine their **Number** and commit to not going beyond it. What's a Number? It's the net worth that pays for the most comfortable lifestyle a person would realistically want to live. And let's be clear that we're talking about the *most comfortable lifestyle:*

telling the wealthy to give everything away and live like monks is counterproductive and unnecessary. Instead, they should figure out exactly what they want and have all of it. But if that only costs X, and someone has a lot more than X, it would be better for them and everyone else if they gave the excess away.

My Number is $100 million, and I'll explain later how I calculated it and why I plan to lower it in the future. A person with very simple tastes might be content with a Number as low as a million dollars. For those on the other end of the spectrum, their Number might be $1–2 billion. Past that, it's all just digits in a bank account, a score in a game. There's zero additional benefit other than bragging rights.

Because here's the thing: it's basically impossible to spend billions of dollars, let alone tens or hundreds of billions. Here's what $1 billion can buy: $200 million in homes around the world, a $100 million mega-yacht, $50 million for a private jet, $50 million for collectibles like art and cars, and $600 million invested generating a minimum of $24 million, and more realistically over $50 million per year—enough to spend nearly $140,000 every single day. That's an absurdly lavish lifestyle and it only costs $1 billion, so what are all the other billions for? Unless they want to take up Competitive Yacht Sinking as a hobby, there is nothing someone with $20 billion can do that someone with $2 billion cannot. We need wealthy people to internalize this truth and begin to put something else above wealth.

For this, I propose three categories of persuasion: altruism, fear, and redirection.

Persuasion by altruism is exactly what it sounds like. It's getting the wealthy to ask themselves honestly what net worth beyond their Number is really achieving. When they do, many will realize this money has no value for them, yet could literally be the difference between life and death for millions of others. They'll see that embracing generosity is not only the morally right thing to do, it leads to a happier and more fulfilled life.

Others will be more persuaded by fear. The US has now reached a level of inequality similar to that of France on the eve of a revolution that saw its monarchs' heads end up in a wicker basket. If you think that can't happen here, consider what already has: Donald Trump's rise was largely a reaction to the perceived excesses of the Left. If inequality keeps on its current trajectory, what's stopping a radical anti-billionaire candidate from taking power? Billionaires are the undisputed winners of *this society*, the one we live in right now. The last thing they should want is any sort of revolution that will replace it with something else, least of all a violent one in a country armed to the teeth.

This brings us to our last group, and it's an especially wealthy one. These are the people for whom growing their net worth delivers meaning, respect, influence, accolades, and a way to pass the time. These are the founders and entrepreneurs whose very identity is inextricably tied up in their businesses. It's totally understandable that these people will not be easily dissuaded from chasing higher net worth, and so we need to find ways to make giving and philanthropy scratch the same itch that accumulating wealth does now. I'll elaborate later on how we do this. For now, think of this as persuasion by redirection.

The ultra wealthy are as logical and reasonable as anyone else. They're not going to respond to demagogues and culture warriors who've never built a business or created a job telling them what pieces of garbage they are, but they will respond to sound arguments.

And they'll take action when there's a clear action to take.

We need something to rally around

One of the many problems with tax policy as a solution to inequality is that it's incredibly weak as a rallying cry. I suppose it would go something like, "Try to elect politicians who promise to raise taxes on rich people (among dozens of other priorities), then hope they'll keep their promises (which politicians rarely do) as they try to pass effective tax laws in a toxic political environment where legislators increasingly can't pass any laws at all."

Huzzah?

Here's my rallying cry: "Make the case directly to the ultra wealthy that it's in their interest to be more generous. Here are the arguments and resources you need to do that."

It's not enough to just propose solutions. Many have done that, but because their proposals mostly rely on government action, they fail when politicians inevitably let us down. Meanwhile, there's nothing the average person can do to help.

My approach is different. With this book, I'm providing a series of clear arguments we can make to the ultra wealthy for why they should voluntarily address inequality themselves. With AboveWealth.org, I'm building a platform to turn these ideas into action. Together, these two resources will provide both the message and the means to solve this problem.

AboveWealth.org allows wealthy people to calculate their Number, access reputable charities, and gain insights into global giving, all with the goal of making generosity aspirational, measurable, and rewarding. Over time, it will evolve into an authoritative source of truth for charitable giving and a marketplace connecting those who have money with those who need it. It will contain a comprehensive database of humanitarian and social problems that need solving, including price tags and completion statuses. Better data and friendly competition will channel the wealthy's energy toward solving big problems, and inspire others to follow.

Here's the plan

Putting all of this together, here's the plan.

First, we wage a massive influence campaign consisting of books (hi!), articles, podcasts, television, social media, and online videos, all directed at getting the wealthy to embrace generosity. The concept of living by one's Number needs to permeate the cultural conversation to such an extent that it can't be avoided. The world's wealthiest people, whose fame has reached a level that was once the exclusive domain of movie stars, should be asked about their Number in every interview. Paragons of generosity like MacKenzie Scott and Chuck Feeney need to become household names.

Second, we need to overhaul the way we think about wealth and generosity. Hitting children was once a cultural default most people accepted without question, yet today is generally seen as a barbaric anachronism—the same evolution must happen with endlessly maximizing net worth. We need to move past the idea of admiring someone simply for being rich and turn today's shrines to wealth (e.g. the Forbes 400 list) into cultural relics. We need to make the wealthy understand that true greatness lies not in obsolete signs of social status, but in generosity. In this world, we could expect Sergey Brin to pay for maternity leave for any American whose employer doesn't cover it, and Larry Page to respond by personally funding worldwide malaria elimination efforts.[4] If this sounds fanciful today, it's only because we've designed every incentive to reward accumulation while treating generosity as an afterthought. It's time to change that.

Much of this book speaks directly to the wealthy, but the target audience is everyone. The ultra wealthy make up less than 0.1% of the population, and very few of them are in the market for a book about why they should give away a large percentage of their money. A book directed solely at them will never be read. But if enough people start talking about these ideas, they'll eventually bubble up to those in a position to act on them, and then real change becomes possible.

The richest people in the world have more than enough money to solve humanity's most intractable problems. Now it's up to us to follow the advice of the venerable Mr. Carnegie: we need to make them *want* to do it.

4. The cost of these things would barely put a dent in Larry and Sergey's net worth.

1

WHAT IS WEALTH AND WHY DO WE HOARD IT?

Here's a thought experiment that illustrates the human instinct to hoard wealth. Imagine you could be placed at a random location on Earth in a random year over the course of human existence. What would you see? What would you experience?

If you were dropped at any point from 300,000 years ago until about 10,000 years ago, you'd see hunter-gatherers whose existence revolved entirely around finding their next meal. You'd see people gorging themselves after a hunt and hiding surplus food underground or in trees, hoping to tide themselves over until their next windfall. This covers roughly 97% of human history. From 10,000 years ago until about 100 years ago, the vast majority of people you met would be subsistence farmers. This is a slightly more predictable existence than hunting and gathering, but droughts and famines were a regular occurrence and could decimate individuals, families, tribes, and entire states at any time. There was no safety net; if the crop failed, you died.

Only if you were dropped in the last 100 years, *and* in a rich and developed country, could you expect to see people spending most of their time on anything other than figuring out their next meal. This is the only time in human history where you would meet a critical mass of people living above the most basic level of subsistence, and even today those people are in the minority. In the undeveloped world, food scarcity is still a real concern. In the developed world, most people spend most of their waking hours working to keep themselves fed, clothed, and sheltered.

Given this context, it makes perfect sense that human beings have a strong instinctive drive to hoard resources, to grab and hold onto as much as they can. It also makes sense that we have no counterbalancing instinct that says "that's enough, I don't need more." Where would such an instinct come from? It would be so maladaptive that if it ever came about by genetic mutation, those unfortunate individuals who possessed it would quickly die out.

Because we each have a strong drive to amass resources, we expect others to do the same. Rich or poor, we're all running the same basic operating system and have the same instincts around scarcity and survival. This is why billionaires go right on building up their net worth past numbers that can't even be conceptualized, and it's why the rest of us don't bat an eye about it. While we may intellectually recognize that such concentration of wealth could be socially harmful or ethically questionable, we don't question the billionaire's desire to amass that wealth in the first place. On a deep, intuitive level, we understand why they're doing it.

What is wealth?

Just as historical context helps us understand the impulse to hoard resources, it's also critical to understanding what wealth actually is. The dictionary tells us that wealth is "an abundance of valuable possessions or resources." But how do we define things like "abundance" or "valuable possessions"? Our conception of these things has changed dramatically over time, and so too has the meaning of wealth.

Mansa Musa, the 14th-century ruler of the Mali Empire, is considered to be the wealthiest person who ever lived. He controlled vast trade and resources, including an abundance of that age-old valuable possession, gold. In fact, he had so much gold that when he made his pilgrimage to Mecca in 1324, he needed hundreds of camels to carry it.

But what could he actually do with that wealth? By modern standards, not that much. No internet, no jet travel, no air conditioning, no modern medicine. Make a list of your most valuable possessions —Mansa Musa had virtually none of them and couldn't even conceive of most of them. What explains this disconnect whereby, in a very real sense, the richest person in history had less than all but the very poorest people living today?

Short answer: the Industrial Revolution, which got started in Great Britain in the late 18th century. From the beginning of human civilization about 10,000 years ago up until this time, daily life for most people changed very little. Progress was glacial. The opportunities and material possessions available to a king from antiquity were much the same as those of a king from 300 years ago—same for everyone else.

And then the Industrial Revolution changed everything. Automation, machinery, and fossil fuels made humans many times more productive than they were before. This meant less time growing food and more time for everything else: scientific and technological breakthroughs, the advent of modern market-based economies, and a host of other things that completely changed how we think and live. These advancements compounded over time, ultimately culminating in the modern era we live in today.

The reason the richest person in history lived a lifestyle that seems unbearably primitive to modern people is that rapid technological progress has elevated our standard of living by orders of magnitude. While we continue to have a substantial gap in relative wealth, with the richest having much more wealth than the poorest, our material standard of living has improved so much that the poorest people today live substantially better lives—in terms of health, longevity, and access to goods and services—than the richest people did even 100 years ago.

So if the richest kings of the past had less wealth than the poorest 1% of people living in the developed world today, what does that say about the richest 1%?

Kings vs. Billionaires

One of the arguments people make to downplay the issue of wealth inequality is that it has always existed and always will because it's hardwired into us, and if you go back in time it used to be even worse. Just compare the medieval king to one of his lowly serfs. Surely that was a much greater level of wealth inequality, so things must be improving, right?

Not quite.

When we look back hundreds of years and see kings wearing silk and jewels while the average peasant slept on a pile of straw with the pigs, it's tempting to think this is a problem that's gradually solving itself. But we need to ask ourselves some important questions. Why did kings hoard wealth? How much wealth did they really have? What could they actually do with it?

The main reason feudal lords amassed wealth was to bolster the strength of their realm, which was a very sensible thing to do. Large kingdoms could grow and conquer smaller kingdoms, and avoid being conquered themselves. If you asked a medieval king why he should accumulate endless wealth, he'd probably say something about it being God's will, then explain the practical reality: "If I don't do it, the king on the other side of that hill will become more powerful than me, and then he'll come over here and kill all of us and take our land." That's a pretty good reason to build wealth! Of course, kings also hoarded for vanity, dynastic power, and personal aggrandizement, but national defense provided a strong justification for never saying "enough is enough."

But just how wealthy were these kings of yore, and how wide was the wealth gap? At the superficial level of silk vs. straw, it might seem quite wide, but when you realize just how little wealth there actually was in the pre-industrial world, a different truth emerges.

Louis IX, who ruled France from 1226 to 1270, was one of the most charitable kings of the Middle Ages. He personally served meals to the poor, washed the feet of lepers, built hospitals and almshouses, and fed more than a hundred people daily at his court. His extraordinary charity and piety led to his canonization in 1297; he remains the only French king ever to be made a saint.

He sets an admirable example, but by modern standards even this most generous of medieval kings really couldn't do much for the average person. While he could build a hospital in Paris, he couldn't send money to the rest of his realm without modern banking. Even locally, direct distributions of coin wouldn't have helped much since agricultural economies had little capacity to absorb sudden wealth. Peasants might have more gold in their purses, but with that money chasing the same limited supply of goods, the result would simply be inflation, not improved living standards. Without mass production and a global economy, there just wasn't the capacity to translate money into meaningful improvements in quality of life.

Now consider the modern equivalent of a medieval king, at least in terms of relative wealth: the billionaire. How do these two stack up?

Whereas the wealth of a medieval king effectively served as an analog for the power of the state, no such link exists for billionaires. Billionaires are not maximizing their wealth for the sake of national defense—we pay taxes for that. While it's true that billionaire-led enterprises serve national interests through innovation, employment, and infrastructure development, these benefits are incidental. They are not the primary purpose of wealth accumulation and do not justify unlimited hoarding the way national defense once did for kings. Whatever wealth a billionaire possesses is his and his alone, with no expectation that he would ever have to use it to muster an army.

The differences in their potential for using their wealth are even more stark. While the vast majority of the kings of France couldn't buy a banana,[1] even the lowliest billionaire, one who's scarcely earned his third comma, has full and unfettered access to the global economy, mass production, and all of the opportunities to spend wealth that those present. With the click of a button, he can instantly improve the lives of millions of people in countless ways. Food, housing, education, sanitation, and medicine can be deployed at scale anywhere in the world.

The moral landscape has also developed significantly over this time. The medieval mind existed in a fog that has burned off since the Enlightenment. In that world, wealth inequality was simply part of the natural state of affairs: kings ruled by divine right, and the pauper's plight was ordained by God. The ultra wealthy of times past had little knowledge of poverty beyond the places they lived, and even less ability or feeling of obligation to do anything about it. By contrast, modern billionaires have access to comprehensive information about global poverty—they know there are hundreds of millions of malnourished people in the world, and few can take solace in chalking that up to God's will. Ancient kings lacked the knowledge, resources, and moral intuitions to do anything about wealth inequality. Modern billionaires lack none of these things.

THE IMPULSE to hoard wealth is rooted in survival instincts as well as practical and ethical barriers to sharing wealth before the modern era. The evolutionary component is hardwired into our brains and will therefore always be with us. Historical precedent isn't quite as inextricable, yet its influence is nevertheless persistent. An implicit part of the justification for amassing wealth is that it's what rich people have always done; today's billionaires are only following the example of yesterday's kings. As illustrated above, there are material differences between these two groups, but they're not immediately apparent and so they're easy to miss.

1. France had kings for about 1,300 years, the last 300 of which also had bananas.

Beyond the two major forces of biology and history, there are a number of other reasons people seek to maximize their wealth. I'll note a few without belaboring the obvious.

Power: Net worth has a fairly linear relationship with power. The more money you have, the more powerful you are. Whether it's political influence, the ability to shape industries, or simply having the freedom to make decisions that affect others, a lot of people like power.

Status: Humans are highly social, and few things bolster a person's social status like wealth. In many circles, net worth becomes a proxy for success, intelligence, and value to society. Maximizing wealth thus doubles as a way of maximizing status, gaining respect from peers, and increasing one's sense of self-worth.

Dopamine: Making money and maximizing net worth "just feels good." It scratches an itch and provides a dopamine hit similar to drugs and alcohol. The thrill of closing a deal, watching investments appreciate, or seeing net worth climb can become genuinely addictive, creating a psychological dependence that has little to do with actual needs.

With so many good reasons to accumulate wealth, it's little wonder that so many people are motivated to do it, and so few ever stop once they've started. The hard truth is that human beings are ill-equipped in deep and various ways to grapple with wealth inequality. Amassing wealth comes from a survival instinct we all possess, and so we naturally struggle to see anything wrong with it. Even as the wealth gap grows ever wider, most people have an intuitive understanding of the billionaire's desire to grow his pile and are more sympathetic to it than arguments for redistributing wealth, which run counter to many of our deepest drives and cultural beliefs.

The good news is that most of the justifications for hoarding wealth can be met with strong counterarguments. The precedent of most wealthy people keeping most of their money can be countered with persuasive arguments rooted in history and economics for why things don't have to stay this way forever. A person's desire for power, status, identity, and dopamine can be satisfied just as effectively—more so in many cases—in other ways that also benefit society.

For all of the good (and not so good) reasons to hoard wealth, there are even more and better reasons to be generous with it. Unfortunately, little effort is made to put forward rational, fact-based arguments for wealthy people to be more generous. Instead, many appeals for redistributing wealth are poorly formulated, fail to grapple with economic reality, or fall on deaf ears because they come from the self-proclaimed enemies of the wealthy class.

I do not see wealthy people as the enemy. As someone who has run businesses and built considerable wealth myself, I understand the mindset, motivations, and concerns of wealthy people. I know their moral compass is as well-calibrated as anyone else's, and that many of them will be open to sound arguments on this topic. The key is to make those arguments persuasively and respectfully, which I aim to do over the following chapters.

If you're a wealthy person, I think this book can provide a blueprint for living a better life, one that maximizes your impact on the world as well as your own happiness and well-being. If you're not wealthy, I hope you'll share these ideas with your friends and family. The more voices join this conversation, the faster it will spread.

2

THE WEALTH GAP

"Software is eating the world."
— Marc Andreessen

If you're trying to solve a problem, it's generally helpful to understand its causes. For all the talk one hears about wealth inequality these days, it's hard to get clear answers on what's driving it, the reasons it's getting worse, and why all of this matters. Let's address that.

Why is the wealth gap widening?

It's impossible to overstate what a gift the Industrial Revolution was for ordinary people. Millions moved from farming to better-paying factory jobs, manufactured goods became affordable, and literacy skyrocketed. Vast personal fortunes were made on the back of all this change, but the more pronounced effect was the rise of the middle class.

The Ford Motor Company was one of the great business success stories of the early 20th century and illustrates this point nicely. Henry Ford famously introduced the $5 workday in 1914, more than doubling the previous daily wage while reducing the workday from nine hours to eight. His aim was to reduce turnover, boost productivity, and attract better talent; as an ancillary benefit, the higher wage meant more people could afford to buy his cars. Ford's employee count climbed from about 65,000 workers in 1920 to 175,000 by 1929, and while efficiency gains boosted per-employee production over that time, the fundamental equation remained: if Ford wanted to produce more cars, he needed to hire more people, purchase more steel, and build more factories. In other words, his business scaled linearly—to double his output, he had to double his inputs.

Building cars this way made Henry Ford spectacularly wealthy—the richest person in the world for a time and history's second billionaire, after John D. Rockefeller. But crucially, Ford couldn't build his fortune alone. He needed armies of workers. He needed steel mills and rubber plants and glass factories, entire supply chains directly employing hundreds of thousands of people, whose wages indirectly supported hundreds of thousands of other jobs. His wealth creation was, by necessity, a rising tide that lifted many boats.

Now let's fast forward to the Internet Revolution and one of its preeminent billionaires, Mark Zuckerberg. Facebook was founded in 2004. By 2007 it had reached global scale while only employing about 300 people, and had a valuation of $15 billion. The company went public in 2012 with 4,600 employees and a valuation of $104 billion.[1] As I write this sentence, Meta is worth about $1.5 trillion.[2]

By comparison, Ford reached a peak in 1929, its 26th year in business, with 175,000 employees and an estimated valuation of around $19 billion in today's dollars. Facebook reached more than five times that value in eight years with just 4,600 employees—that's 2.6% as

1. Coincidentally, this is very close to the highest market cap Ford ever hit, $103.3 billion in January 2022.

2. Facebook changed its name to Meta in 2021.

many people generating about 208 times more value per employee: $22.6 million versus $109,000.

Why such a huge difference?

One word: software. Henry Ford needed massive investment, infrastructure, and manpower to get his business off the ground; Mark Zuckerberg needed only himself and a computer. Ford was famous for bringing down costs with innovations like the assembly line, but that only went so far; while the cost to build his millionth car was less than his first, it was still substantial. Facebook's first, millionth, and billionth user all had a marginal cost measured in fractions of a cent.

Software businesses, especially network-based ones, scale very differently from old economy businesses, i.e. ones that rely heavily on tangible physical assets. Once software is built, it can be replicated infinitely and sent anywhere in the world for nearly zero incremental cost. It would be like Ford building a single car, selling it millions of times, and shipping it anywhere in the world instantly for a few cents.

Also, unlike physical products, network products actually get better as more people use them. Compare this to something like a gym. As more people join a gym, it gets crowded and run-down and the experience gets worse. Eventually, the owner has to open a new location for a substantial investment—new lease, new equipment, new employees—which increases costs.

By comparison, Facebook's value proposition is connecting you to other people, and so the more users it has, the more valuable it becomes. Not only do these incremental users cost Facebook nothing, they make the product better, increasing time on the platform, which in turn increases its advertising revenues. Google benefits from a similar network effect. The more users it has, the more indispensable it becomes to advertisers. More users also means more data to improve search results, driving even more customers, searches, and revenue. Ford and 24 Hour Fitness can't outrun their costs and sell a product whose value can only decline (depreciating cars, crowded gyms); Facebook and Google get new users for free, and each one makes the value of their product increase, allowing them to charge more for it. This fundamental difference in how their businesses scale explains why today's billionaires are so much wealthier than yesterday's, and why they employ far fewer people.

The venture capitalist Marc Andreessen, an early investor in Facebook, wrote in a 2011 essay that "software is eating the world," and this is why. No other business comes close in its ability to scale or create wealth. When the Internet Revolution kicked off around 1995, only one out of the ten highest market cap companies in the US (IBM) was what we would consider a technology company. Thirty years later, every single one is a technology company.

The effect on wealth distribution is plain to see. The Industrial Revolution reduced inequality by moving large numbers of people a couple rungs up the wealth ladder, from poverty to the middle class. The Internet Revolution increased inequality by moving a much smaller group many more rungs up the ladder, mostly from middle to upper class. A lucky few blasted off past the ladder to a space station orbiting Earth.

Of course, the shift from an industrial to an information economy is not the only driver of wealth inequality today. Globalization has moved high-paying middle and working class jobs offshore, driving up wages in developing countries while depressing them in the US.[3] The top marginal tax rate has declined from 70% in the 1960s to 37% today, boosting not just the take-home pay of top earners but their ability to invest and compound that wealth over decades. The decline of labor unions and the rise of financialization have also played a role.

I don't want to downplay any of these causes, and if not for the "get to the bloody point" ethos of this book, I might be tempted to discuss them at length. However, I'm primarily focused on solutions to our current situation, and that end is not served by a long-winded analysis of every driver of the problem. This is especially true when

3. It should be noted, however, that automation and robots have taken far more American jobs than overseas workers. Even here, it's all about technology.

one considers that these things are mostly here to stay, as in every case reversing them is either impossible, impractical, or undesirable.

As much as we may occasionally pine for simpler pre-internet times or feel like throwing our phones out the window, very few people would willingly give up technology, which is just as well since that option is not on the table. It's the same with globalization, which has mostly been a positive even if it has contributed to inequality at the margins. It's possible that a resurgence in labor unions could help reduce inequality for certain types of workers, but its effect on the overall problem would be minimal, and unions come with significant downsides of their own. As for taxes, we should absolutely reform the tax code to make billionaires pay their fair share, but doing so presents so many challenges that I devoted most of Chapter 6 to laying them out; for now I'll just say that raising taxes is not the silver bullet many people think it is.

There are two reasons I've mostly focused on the shift from a pre- to a post-digital economy as a driver of inequality. First, the rise of the technology sector and relative decline of everything else dwarfs all other drivers of modern wealth inequality. Net worths in the tens of billions were unheard of before the internet boom; today we see fortunes in the hundreds of billions (with one over a trillion), and tech founders and investors dominate the Forbes 400 just as tech companies dominate the stock market. These gargantuan fortunes were built with a fraction of the manpower of those of the 20th century while simultaneously automating out of existence many middle and working class jobs.

The second is that spreading awareness of this fact actually does serve a practical purpose. People need to understand that upward wealth concentration is an intrinsic feature of the companies that drive the modern economy, and AI is only going to accelerate the trend. When politicians say they can address inequality by onshoring manufacturing jobs, they're either misguided or lying. Proposed solutions to wealth inequality that don't account for this tectonic shift in our economy will never work and should not be entertained.

Addressing inequality requires tech founders and financiers to realize that while they have been the winners of this economy, it could all backfire. Only so much wealth can move from the middle to the upper class before societal instability becomes inevitable. That means the ultra wealthy need to take the initiative and start working to reduce inequality themselves, before it's too late.

A growing divide that hurts everyone

In the last chapter, we discussed how the poorest people today live substantially better lives than rich people in the not-too-distant past. This begs the question: does wealth inequality even matter? After all, if a modern poor person has more opportunities and material comforts (e.g. access to vaccines, jet travel, and endless entertainment via their smartphone) than a rich person of the early 20th century, what is the actual problem here? It would seem that things are getting better all around, and even if the poor have less than the rich, they still have more than their grandparents and every other human who came before them.

While there's some truth to this argument, it doesn't change the fact that rising inequality is doing real damage to society. A low-income person in 21st century America has many things that John D. Rockefeller didn't have, but her lack of wealth relative to the top 1% presents a variety of problems not only for her but for the wealthy themselves.

To start, wealth inequality is demoralizing for working and middle class people. It erodes trust, social cohesion, and democratic participation, and increases stress and anxiety. Social media exacerbates all of this. Open Instagram and it won't be long before you see someone with a huge house and fancy car flying around to exotic locations on a private jet. This is a hard pill to swallow for the average person struggling to buy a modest home, or just pay rent, despite doing everything they were told would lead to success.

Unsurprisingly, we see that Gen Z—who have spent their entire lives in the post-digital economy and on social media—feel this disconnect more acutely than any other generation. When asked in a recent survey what salary they would need to consider themselves a financial success, their answer was by far the highest: $588,000, compared to $181,000 for Millennials, $212,000 for Gen X, and $100,000 for Baby Boomers.[4] In the same survey, 65% of Gen Z respondents said they feel they're starting further behind financially than prior generations at the same age.

Gen Z's sky-high expectations reflect a mixture of fantasy and hard reality. From the time they were children, they've had over-the-top wealth shoved in their faces on social media, vastly inflating their sense of what a reasonable income is. But now as adults, they face the least affordable housing market in recent history, and in this context their high estimation of financial success looks less like delusions of grandeur and more like doing the math. Whatever one thinks about their expectations, when you combine the feeling of needing to make more than half a million per year with the belief you'll never get anywhere near that amount, it's a recipe for an entire generation losing hope in the American Dream.

Speaking of which, that dream is another victim of growing wealth inequality. One of the bedrock principles that made America the most prosperous nation in history was the promise of social and economic mobility. In the Old World, it was "what school did you go to?" or "who's your father?" Here, anyone with brains, backbone, and a strong work ethic could get ahead, and there was no limit to how high you could go. This idea compelled millions of people, including my father, to leave their places of birth and seek opportunity here, and it made the United States the world's largest importer of ambitious and talented people.

What happens when people don't hold that belief anymore? America loses its dynamism. Sergey Brin, Elon Musk, and countless other founders didn't start their businesses in the countries they came from. They started them here. If people stop believing America is the best place in the world to get ahead, the next generation of

---

4. https://fortune.com/2024/11/23/gen-z-financial-success-definition-salary-net-worth-millennials-gen-x-boomers/

founders will be less likely to move here and the US will gradually start to look more like the old colonial powers of Europe—still relatively wealthy and influential, sure, but no longer the center of the world.

Another effect of the widening wealth gap is a loss of political power and financial prospects for middle and working class people. This makes them more susceptible to demagogues promising simple solutions to complex problems. Every election becomes a referendum on the last guy who couldn't deliver what he promised, with political power swinging between ever more polarized parties. People eventually get fed up and become more likely to vote for extreme candidates. This is how Germany, the most advanced and tolerant country in early 1930s Europe, ended up electing Adolf Hitler and plunging the globe into the most destructive war in history. We ignore this history at our peril.

Finally, wealth inequality could very well break the economy as we know it, and there's strong evidence this is already under way. Gary Stevenson, a former Citibank trader who made millions betting on economic stagnation, speaks quite compellingly on this subject. His thesis is fairly technical, but I'll do my best to summarize it here.

Working people spend nearly all their income on goods and services, which keeps money flowing through the economy. By contrast, rich people save and invest most of their income because they have more than enough to cover their basic needs. When wealth concentrates at the top, we have too much savings and not enough spending to drive economic growth, which keeps wages and interest rates perpetually low. Yet all that saved money has to go somewhere, so it floods into assets like housing and stocks, driving up prices. Working wages stay low as a result of an anemic economy, but housing gets more expensive as wealthy people bid up prices. The middle class gets squeezed from both sides, earning less while assets cost more, making it nearly impossible to build wealth no matter how hard they work. Meanwhile, rich people take advantage of low interest rates to acquire more stocks and real estate, driving the prices of those assets ever higher.

Consider a young couple trying to buy their first home. Their wages have barely budged in ten years, but housing prices have doubled because wealthy investors are bidding up real estate. They're stuck renting forever and can never build wealth through homeownership as previous generations did, despite working full-time jobs.

In the short run, this is bad for the poor and good for the rich. In the long run, it's bad for everyone. Consumer spending accounts for 70% of the US economy and similar proportions across most Western nations. As the middle class gets squeezed due to stagnant wages and unaffordable housing, they don't spend as much on Amazon or at the mall. Less spending leads to companies pulling back on advertising, hitting Google and Facebook, and eventually layoffs, which means fewer Microsoft Office subscriptions. Stock valuations are expressed in multiples of revenue and earnings, and so the decline in these companies' operations gets expressed many times over in terms of their stock prices, which implode. Centi-billionaires become mere billionaires.

Even the wealthiest people in the world depend on a functioning economy, and that economy requires people to have enough money to keep the engine running. There is a point at which the entire thing breaks down, and the ultra wealthy should care more than anyone about preventing that. It's hard to enjoy one's billions in the chaos of an economic collapse.

And this brings us to the most counterintuitive victim of inequality: wealthy people. While on a superficial level, it would seem that all of this is working out great for them—and to be clear, it's certainly going better for them than everyone else—they don't escape unscathed.

Research shows that money can buy happiness up to a point, but the returns taper off pretty quickly and past a certain level they're nearly zero.[5] If you're worth $100 million, you're not going to be much

5. https://www.hbs.edu/ris/Publication%20Files/donnelly%20zheng%20haisley%20norton_26bec744-c924-4a28-8439-5a74abe9c8da.pdf

happier at $200 million, and the difference is even smaller going from $1 billion to $2 billion.

What *does* actually make you happier? The #1 predictor across nearly every study is deep, meaningful relationships.[6] Too bad, then, that it's so lonely at the top. Aggregating wealth tends to work against strong relationships, and the higher you go, the lonelier it gets, with billionaires being some of the most isolated people in the world. They're surrounded by bodyguards, yes-men, and people seeking power and favors—not friends. They can't go out and be an anonymous person in society, and having normal relationships is extremely difficult. When we see some ultra wealthy people displaying antisocial behavior or a lack of empathy, this likely has a lot to do with it.

Now, a lot of this isolation is the unfortunate price of extreme celebrity, and I'm not suggesting that being more generous obviates the need for bodyguards. But generosity does open doors to human connection that wealth alone keeps shut. Bill Gates was a notoriously ruthless businessman, a difficult boss, and not particularly well-liked by the public as he was building Microsoft. His public image improved dramatically when he shifted his focus to philanthropy, and he has described the work as deeply fulfilling. This is not at all surprising. There can be no doubt that he's learned more, had more rewarding experiences, and forged more meaningful relationships in the battle against AIDS and polio than he would have if he'd devoted the last twenty years to growing Microsoft's share price.

What else drives happiness? The data say that after relationships, the second and third spots are held by agency and purpose.

Agency is one of the defining characteristics that separate the wealthy from everyone else, a truth succinctly captured by the term "fuck you money." Unlike people of ordinary means, who often have to work jobs they hate in order to pay the bills, the ultra wealthy have enough money to do whatever they want. The irony is that many

6. https://news.harvard.edu/gazette/story/2017/04/over-nearly-80-years-harvard-study-has-been-showing-how-to-live-a-healthy-and-happy-life/; https://ccare.stanford.edu/press_posts/good-social-relationships-are-the-most-consistent-predictor-of-a-happy-life/

express their agency by choosing to continue growing their net worth, which often shackles them to their current role and reduces their options for how they spend their time. For these people, maximizing agency is in conflict with maximizing net worth, and they'd be better off stopping at a net worth that covers their optimal lifestyle—their Number, in other words.

Purpose is more interesting. It's certainly possible to derive purpose and meaning from one's work, and many entrepreneurs would say building their business does precisely that. Fair enough, but there's no reason this has to be incompatible with generosity. Building a business provides purpose, but the excess billions sitting in the bank do not. There's nothing stopping a dyed-in-the-wool entrepreneur from spending all his time and energy growing his business empire while giving away the excess money he's never going to spend. He can derive meaning from his work while also being a force for good and doing his part to narrow the wealth gap.

3

HOW MONEY ACTUALLY WORKS

"Nothing succeeds like success."
— Alexandre Dumas[1]

One of my earliest memories is the first conversation I ever had about money.

"Okay, Johnny, you have one dollar, and I have two, so together we have three. A Nintendo costs 100 dollars, so we only need 97 more dollars."

I was five or six, so my little brother, Johnny, must have been about four. I don't remember how we came into the three dollars, but the rest of the money came from lemonade stands, chores, begging, the usual kid stuff. Eventually we got the Nintendo, I don't remember how long it took.

As a kid, money was a scarce resource whose quantity vacillated between zero and double digits, occasionally breaking into three-digit territory after Christmas or a birthday. I was a saver even from

1. This adage is generally attributed to Dumas, though it likely predates him.

an early age, but I never had much of it. The entirety of my wealth lived in a blue velcro wallet, which never got too fat before the money was spent on toys, candy, a bike, or playing Mortal Kombat II at 7-Eleven.

From childhood until the time I started making real money in my late twenties, I thought about money in a certain way. I needed a minimum amount of it for my needs and wants, my store of money would deplete as I spent it on those things, and when my bank account balance got too low, I'd think, "Shit, I need more money."

This is how many people think about money for their entire lives; rich people do not think about money this way.

But before we get to that, here's another childhood thought: "If I had $10 million, I'd buy a mansion for $4 million and then I'd buy some awesome cars and a bunch of other rad stuff for $1 million, and I'd still have $5 million left over!"[2]

Okay, enough memory lane. Here's how a rich person would think about this: "If I have $10 million, my money is earning between $400,000 and $1 million per year."

As I write this sentence, a money market fund, which is effectively the safest liquid investment a person can make, yields about 4%; the historic average annual return of the S&P 500 is about 10%. Therefore, a $10 million investment can yield $400,000 in annual income with essentially zero risk, and a smarter and more balanced investment strategy will get you closer to $1 million. Depending on where you live, this income will most likely be tax-advantaged relative to income from wages.

You can live very comfortably—raising a family, living in a big house, and going on nice vacations—with an annual income in this range. And each year, any money you don't spend gets added to the initial $10 million and starts earning a return. For example, if you had $200,000 left over after expenses and taxes, you'd now be earning income off of $10.2 million. This is called compounding.[3]

2. My childhood thoughts were in pre-inflation 1990s dollars.

3. *The Snowball*, a 2008 biography of Warren Buffett, is named after a metaphor for

And we're only talking about $10 million here. Let's split the difference on this range and assume a 7% annual return: $100 million earns $7 million annually, $10 billion earns $700 million, and so on. Don't forget that this compounds, meaning that net worth goes up by any unspent money, which further increases annual income. Also, at these higher levels of net worth, banks will issue what's called a margin loan, allowing a wealthy person to borrow against the value of their assets at a low interest rate. If they sold assets to cover living expenses, they would incur a tax bill and no longer earn a return from whatever they sold. With the margin loan, they avoid taxes, continue earning returns that generally exceed the loan's interest rate, and can further lower their taxes by writing off the interest on the loan.

This is how money works.

Once your net worth gets high enough you can afford a lifestyle ranging from comfortable to ludicrously extravagant just from your investment income; there's no need to dip into the money you started with, aka your net worth. Speaking for myself, I would never dream of doing that. The idea of spending so much money that my net worth would actually go down is almost unthinkable.

Bringing this back to my childhood conception of money for a moment, I did not realize money worked this way until I was wealthy. I thought of wealthy people as having a certain amount of money, just like me, except the number was bigger. They'd spend it on their mansion, rocket car, and Scrooge McDuck Money Bin, and eventually they'd run out of it, just like me.

Nope. Not at all. Not even close.

While it's possible for an ultra wealthy person to spend so much that their net worth declines or even goes to zero, it's rare.[4] What is far more common is that a wealthy person's fortune earns enough to fund their lifestyle, with enough left over to increase their earnings

---

compounding. Buffett grew his fortune from compound interest in the same way a snowball gets larger as it rolls down a hill.

4. Note the word "spend." It's certainly possible for billionaires to go broke from bad investments, but that's not what we're talking about here.

over time such that their net worth climbs ever higher. Tech entrepreneur and NYU professor Scott Galloway calls this "reaching economic escape velocity," and it's an apt metaphor. At some point, your wealth breaks the bonds of daily expenses and generates returns that mean you never have to come back to Earth.

Most people never really think about this, which creates the perception of enormous fortunes being more finite than they really are. In many conversations, I've tried to illustrate how unspendable a fortune in the tens or hundreds of billions of dollars is, only to be countered with, "Well you can't be certain of that, it depends on how expensive the person's lifestyle is."

No, it doesn't.

First, actually spending billions of dollars per year as an individual is nearly impossible even if you're actively trying to be wasteful. Don't get fooled by nine-figure price tags: penthouses, yachts, and private jets are all assets with resale value, and so their only costs are from maintenance and depreciation (in the case of real estate, it's usually gains from appreciation). Open a spreadsheet and try to imagine a lifestyle that costs billions per year, and you'll quickly see that you can't. Second, even if we grant that a multi-billion dollar per year lifestyle is possible, it would still be the case that anyone with that kind of money would be financing their lifestyle from returns, not principal. It's technically possible that someone with billions of dollars could find a way to spend down their net worth, but it's such an outlier scenario as to be the exception that proves the rule.

If the general public understood this, it would dispel the myth that billionaires continue to amass wealth because they need more money to fund their lifestyle. It's one thing to think of a wealthy person's net worth the way regular people think about their own money—as an exhaustible resource that will deplete unless one constantly accumulates. It's another to understand that most ultra wealthy people cannot come close to spending the income their wealth generates, let alone dipping into the principal, and so they can only get more wealthy.

More examples of how money actually works

Remember earlier when I was so adamant about getting to the bloody point? This is where it gets tough, because there's so much to say about how money works and all the implications this has for wealth inequality. But for the sake of brevity, I'll once again stick to just a few examples.

Cost of capital

In the last chapter, I explained how software is eating the world. But wouldn't you know it, I actually understated its appetite. Another way it's eating the world is by driving up the cost of capital for all other industries, and it's pretty easy to understand why. "Cost of capital" is a finance term defined as the minimum rate of return a company must earn to justify an investment. Think of it as the annual return an investor requires to put money into something.

If investors know tech stocks will reliably have much higher returns than anything else, what does that mean for other investments they might make? It means they're going to require a higher rate of return. Before the tech boom, an investor might have been happy to extend a loan or buy an equity stake in a company that yielded an annual return of 9%. But if they know a tech stock will almost certainly earn far more than that, why would they make this investment instead of just investing more in the tech company? They won't. They'll require a higher interest rate on a loan, or if they're buying equity they'll demand to own a larger percentage of the company.

This is one of the more subtle ways the Internet Revolution subverted other industries. Suddenly, all other investments looked far less attractive, meaning investors demanded more onerous terms or simply didn't invest at all. At precisely the time when traditional industries needed more investment—to compete in a world where globalization was making the playing field more competitive than ever before—the response from Wall Street was, "it'll cost ya."

Something similar happened in the labor market. With their stocks going to the moon, tech companies were able to lure the most talented workers away from other sectors. As they aggregated the best talent, tech companies performed better and got more valuable, attracting even more top talent—a virtuous cycle for them and a vicious one for everyone else.

This is another way that money works. It flows into whatever makes the best return, and out of whatever doesn't. As we try to understand how the US economy shifted so rapidly from analog to digital, this is a factor that can't be ignored. And, of course, it's yet another reason why tech founders and investors have been so ascendant relative to everyone else.

Sequestering wealth

Imagine the world's smallest economy: 100 people living on an island. Ninety-nine people make about $50,000 per year, and one person makes 100 times more than everyone else, $5 million per year—let's say she owns most of the real estate on the island and earns money from rent. To start out, the 99 middle class people spend about 60% of their income, with the rest going to savings and taxes. The wealthy person spends a quarter as much as a percentage, 15%, but because her income is 100 times higher, she spends 25 times more than anyone else.

If you do the math, you'll see that about 20% of the spending in the economy comes from this one person. The money she spends is income for everyone else—grocers, farmers, merchants, restaurateurs, personal trainers, landscapers, artists, and so on. The sales tax she pays helps to fund the police, fire department, and schools.

Now let's imagine that she decides one day to reduce her spending from 15% to 5%. What would happen?

Well, total spending would drop by $500,000, which means the economy would shrink by a bit more than 13%. The businesses where the rich woman spends money would see their revenue shrink; in some cases, they may have to lay off workers. The business owners and laid off workers now have less money to spend, which means less income for everyone else; ninety-nine people on the island get poorer.

Meanwhile, the rich woman is now richer. With the money she's no longer spending she can buy more real estate, and as she controls more of the market, she's able to charge higher rents. It's also easier for her to outbid other homebuyers, driving up prices. This is the Gary Stevenson thesis in miniature—one percent of the economy gets ever wealthier, while the rest can't compete and gradually decline.

Now, this is obviously an extreme simplification of how the economy works, but the general point still stands. The more wealth we sequester, the less there is to flow through the economy to create wealth for everyone else; when we spend more, it creates jobs, income, and wealth for everyone else. While most calls to reduce inequality understandably focus on paying a fair tax rate or giving to charity, we shouldn't forget that wealthy people can also reduce the gap by simply spending money on things they enjoy.

This raises an interesting point. The media and popular opinion love to heap scorn on celebrity weddings and other ostentatious displays of wealth, but maybe they have it backwards. Yes, these spectacles are often tacky and distasteful, but they put money in the pockets of the middle class. Unlike those who hoard their cash without ever spending it, the people funding these extravagances are at least spreading the wealth, if only a little bit.

Asset bubbles

I live in San Francisco, a city with one of the highest concentrations of billionaires in the world. In the northwest corner of the city is a neighborhood called Sea Cliff, which boasts stunning views of the Golden Gate Bridge and Pacific Ocean and has been the home of many rich and famous people, including Jack Dorsey, Robin Williams, Kirk Hammett (of Metallica), Ansel Adams, and Sharon Stone.

Let's imagine a Sea Cliff mansion goes up for sale, and three local billionaires want it: Mark Zuckerberg, Jensen Huang, and Laurene Powell Jobs. The property originally lists for $15 million, but a bidding war ensues, and it ultimately ends up going to Zuckerberg for $25 million—no big deal, that's only 0.01% of his net worth.[5]

Here's the question: how much is that property worth?

Easy, right? It's worth $25 million.

Okay, but now consider the fact that when this neighborhood was first built 120 years ago, the most expensive homes sold for less than $500,000 in inflation-adjusted dollars. Has Sea Cliff gotten 50 times better since then, or is there another explanation?

Premium real estate in places like Sea Cliff, Manhattan, and Aspen always has and always will be owned by the richest people in society. But the astronomical price increases we've seen over the last twenty years are not a function of something intrinsic about the land or the homes that sit on it. It's purely a function of wealth concentrating at the top.

Imagine that the United States returned to a wealth distribution closer to what we saw in the mid-20th century. Who lives in Sea Cliff now?

Answer: the exact same people. In this scenario, it's probably the same three billionaires bidding on the mansion—it just ends up selling for $10 million instead of $25 million. In a world of greater generosity, all those beautiful homes in Sea Cliff would still be there, and developers would still be building penthouses in Manhattan. The only difference is that the people bidding on them would have smaller fortunes, and so the properties would have smaller price tags. That difference in price—tens of millions of dollars in some cases—would be circulating in the economy and benefiting everyone, instead of being tied up in one man's house.

---

5. Note the decimal—that's zero-point-zero-one percent, or 1 divided by 10,000. For the median American household with a net worth of $176,500, that's $17.65, almost enough for a large pizza.

WE COVERED a lot of ground in this chapter—saving up for Nintendos, putting money to work, capital allocation, Econ 101 thought experiments, and premium real estate—but the common theme is that nothing succeeds like success. Once you're ahead, barriers and impediments start to melt away and it becomes easier and easier to get richer and richer.

At a certain level of wealth, investment returns cover all your expenses, and any amount left over compounds and increases your wealth even further.

At a certain level of investment return, tech companies are able to suck capital and talent out of other industries, further juicing their returns while traditional industries decline.

When wealthy people cut back on spending, their fortunes quickly rise while everyone else does worse.

And, as a tiny minority accumulates vast wealth, they use it to bid up scarce assets that previously sold for far less, with the difference sitting idle instead of creating wealth for others.

The other common thread is that the ultra wealthy have far more money than they need. That doesn't mean someone should come along and try to take their money away, which is a bad idea for many reasons that I'll get into later. But it does mean there's an opportunity to show them that they can have all of the same material comforts they currently enjoy while also contributing to a society that's happier, safer, and more vibrant.

For this to happen, wealthy people need to know their Number.

4

WHAT'S YOUR NUMBER?

"True abundance flows from enough; never from more."
— Lynne Twist

A primary aim of this book is to introduce a new question into the cultural conversation: "What's your Number?" We currently measure a wealthy person by how much they've managed to accumulate—their net worth. A more interesting question is where they decide to stop.

To recap, I define a person's Number as "the net worth that pays for the most comfortable lifestyle a person would realistically want to live." I've chosen these words deliberately, so let's break them down to make sure there's no confusion.

"**Pays for**" refers to the annual income generated by a given level of net worth; it does not mean spending down one's net worth. For example, $100 million earning a 5% return pays for a $5 million per year lifestyle while maintaining a net worth of $100 million.

"**Most comfortable lifestyle**" is another way of saying "have everything you want." Wealthy people should have an honest conversation with their family and themselves about the experiences and material possessions they really want to have. Fancy vacations, sports cars, luxury goods, private jet travel—whatever it is, figure out what it costs and make sure your Number covers it.

"Realistically" is there to keep people honest. One man cannot realistically drive fifty cars or live in a dozen houses, and while it's perfectly reasonable to want a private jet, he's not going to use it every day. As people formulate their Number, they should be realistic about the things they want and how much they actually cost.

Why your Number matters

One of the central tenets of this book is that there is no good reason to allow your net worth to exceed your Number. The rationale for this is very simple: if you're never going to use it, there's no reason to keep it, and a lot of good you could do by giving it away.

And yet virtually no one does this. Why?

As we explored in Chapter 1, there are strong evolutionary and historical influences at play, as well as the desire for power, status, and dopamine. Yet another reason, which we'll touch on below, is the desire to create dynastic wealth that can be passed down to future generations.

Equally important is the near total absence of pressure in the opposite direction. If a billionaire asks herself whether she'd like her net worth to rise from $2 billion to $3 billion, there are a few reasons to say yes: having more of a good thing feels better than having less; her family's future will be more secure; she can have more power and influence in the world; she'll finally be richer than so-and-so.

As for reasons to say no, there really aren't any. Will she face public backlash? No, most people will expect her to continue amassing wealth, and the anti-billionaire faction won't hate her any more than they already do. What about pushback from her peers? No, they're all maximizing their net worth as well. And her financial advisors? They have a fiduciary duty to grow her wealth.

As long as all of the incentives point toward "amass more wealth," that's exactly what people are going to do. If we want to change this, we need to reverse some of these incentives, and that's where the Number comes in.

Beyond helping wealthy people quantify their actual needs, the Number also serves a cultural purpose. It marks a spot on the number line between $0 and infinite wealth where we start to challenge a person's motivations for going further, a point where they can expect to start meeting real societal resistance. It also gets people out of an "I'll be generous later" mindset and fosters accountability by making generosity a matter of public commitment rather than private intention.

When we don't have a Number, there's no obvious place to stop amassing wealth, and so most people are going to say yes to that extra billion dollars. When we have one, we've committed to a stopping point, and the reasons to say no become much more clear.

Calculating your Number

There are two components to your Number: 1) the annual cost of your lifestyle, and 2) the net worth that generates enough income to pay for that lifestyle. At AboveWealth.org, you'll find a tool ("Calculate Your Number") that makes it easy to figure this out. First, it asks some questions about the nature of your net worth to determine the total **annual return** it generates. Then, it takes you through all of the things you might spend money on—everything from groceries to private jets—to help determine your annual **lifestyle cost.** Finally, it returns your **Number**, the net worth that generates a total annual return that covers your lifestyle cost.[1] There are a few other details—including the concepts of **buffer** and **giving factor**, which I'll explain through the examples below—but that's the gist of it.

In this section, we're going to look at three hypothetical wealthy

1. Note that your Number scales directly with inflation. If inflation causes your lifestyle cost to increase by X% over a period of time, your Number would also increase by X%.

people and discuss the unique considerations for each as they calculate their Number. My hope is that this answers a lot of questions while avoiding a tedious slog through stock portfolios and household budgets.

Without further ado, please meet three different breeds of rich person:

Ben is 30 years old and just sold his tech startup for $100 million. After paying taxes, he has a net worth of $60 million, all in cash.

Clare is 60 years old, has four grown children, and owns a large stake in a chain of hotels, valued at $300 million. She also has other assets—stocks, real estate, art, and so on—bringing her total net worth to $600 million.

Max is the 40 year-old founder of a large tech company. While he owns a variety of assets, 95% of his net worth is in his company's publicly traded stock. His net worth is $60 billion.

While all three of these people are wealthy, they're quite different in terms of their stage of life and the nature of their wealth. How should each of them think about their Number?

Ben

Before we calculate Ben's Number, let's fill in a few more details. Ben worked incredibly hard from the age of sixteen building his business, and as a result he missed out on a lot. He didn't party, didn't travel, didn't take great care of himself, and only recently started his first serious relationship. He also never had much money because his startup wasn't profitable, and so he could only afford to pay himself a modest salary. And, while he's been very risk-aggressive with respect to his business, he remembers his parents losing most of their nest egg during the 2008 financial crisis, and so he's skittish about owning too many stocks.

Now that he's suddenly rich, he wants to make up for a lot of lost living. Here are some of the things he wants to do over the next year: propose to his girlfriend and have a big wedding; travel frequently, flying first class or private and staying in nice hotels; buy an $8 million house ($2 million in equity, $6 million mortgage) in Orange County and decorate it with upscale art; and refurbish his wardrobe and get in shape. He runs the numbers and estimates that his desired **lifestyle cost** is $1.5 million per year. Because he lives in California and pays an effective tax rate of about 50%, he needs to earn $3 million if he wants to net $1.5 million.

Now let's see where this $3 million per year will come from. After buying his house, art, a couple cars, and some other items, he has $57 million remaining to invest. If he put all of that into the S&P 500, which historically returns around 10% per year, his investment income would be $5.7 million. But remember that he wants to invest conservatively, and so he decides to allocate much of his net worth to safe but low-yielding Treasury bonds, resulting in an **annual return** of 6%, or $3.4 million per year.

Okay, what's his Number?

To earn $3 million off of a 6% return, he'd need about $50 million in income-generating assets; adding the $2 million of equity in his house, which doesn't generate income, his **Number** is about $52 million. We established above that his net worth is $60 million, so the next question we must ask ourselves is whether he should give away $8 million, or keep it as a **buffer** and decide that his Number is $60 million.

My opinion is that a reasonable person could go either way, and it's ultimately a personal decision. If Ben wants to follow the Number concept to the letter and not keep a single dollar he doesn't need, he would give it away. If he prefers to maintain a small buffer, that's also totally defensible. What if he's faced with major unexpected expenses? What if there's a market crash? What if we enter a period of inflation? What if he's just not comfortable having his expenses be exactly equal to his income?

I imagine most people who go through the Number exercise will want a buffer for exactly these reasons, and that's fine. As we try to get wealthy people to embrace these ideas, we must always remember not to let the perfect be the enemy of the good. If someone wants to have a Number that's 15–30% higher than what they technically need, that's still much better than not having a Number at all. As long as they're using their buffer to protect against genuine uncertainty—and not to simply inflate their Number—I think it's a reasonable thing to do.

If Ben decides that his Number is $60 million, his $8 million buffer will generate $240,000 per year in post-tax income. When he re-runs the Number exercise at the end of the year, and assuming his lifestyle cost was indeed $1.5 million, he'll have an extra $240,000 that he can give away.

Clare

The Ben example went into the nitty-gritty details of lifestyle cost, annual return, and buffer. To avoid repetition with Clare and Max, we're going to skip over things we already covered and just focus on what's unique about their situation.

Clare grew up modestly wealthy before inheriting her father's hotel business and growing it into a massive success. The value of her stake in the hotel chain has risen steadily over the years, and her investments in stocks and real estate have appreciated significantly as well. Before his death, Clare and her father would often talk about the importance of keeping the business in the family, and how Clare's four children would take over some day. Now retired, she and her husband spend about $3 million per year, which is dwarfed by the $40+ million per year return they make off their $600 million fortune.

After reading this book, Clare realizes that she has more money than she needs and could have the exact same lifestyle with a much lower net worth. Also, given the evidence she's seen of the potential harmful effects of large inheritances on a person's mental health, she no longer wishes to bequeath her entire stake in the family business to her four children. She decides to downsize her wealth to a level that will generate $7 million per year in pre-tax income for herself and her husband; net of taxes, this will cover her $3 million lifestyle cost with a $500,000 buffer. She's also going to follow Warren

Buffett's advice on inheritance by leaving her children "enough so they can do anything, but not enough that they can do nothing."

In order to maintain diversification, she reduces her net worth evenly across her various assets: she maintains her primary residence and one vacation home, and sells the rest of her real estate; she sells most of her stocks; and, she transfers a large chunk of her economic interest in the family business to a charitable foundation, structuring the transaction to retain her voting rights and control over the company. In the end, she reduces her net worth to $100 million (her Number), gives each of her four children $15 million, and donates $440 million to various charitable causes.

One way to quantify her giving is to say it's 4.4x, or 440%, of her net worth. If she wants to express her net worth in a way that captures the fact that she has intentionally capped it and given away the excess, she could say she has a net worth of $100 million with a 440% **giving factor**, which we might write as $100m/440g.[2]

There are two important takeaways from Clare's situation. First, even people who are "only" worth hundreds of millions of dollars—keep in mind we've mostly been talking about billionaires so far—can still have vastly more wealth than they will ever spend, allowing them to give away much or most of it while continuing to live exactly the same lifestyle. Second, people who go on amassing enormous fortunes so they can give it to their children should really think twice. The Vanderbilts may be the most famous example of the pitfalls of large family inheritances, but there is plenty of other evidence to suggest that you're not doing your children any favors by leaving them a massive fortune they haven't earned; the Chapter Notes section of Appendix A contains further reading on this topic.

---

2. As we try to persuade the wealthy to be more generous, spreading the concept of giving factor does a lot of work for very little effort. For many people, their wealth is an important part of their self-conception, and in today's culture there's only one metric that captures it: net worth. Unsurprisingly, we see that this is exactly what the ultra wealthy compete over. The simple inclusion of giving factor alongside net worth conveys enormous meaning and creates a more socially constructive way to signal wealth. When someone has a high giving factor relative to their net worth, they're making a clear and powerful statement about what they truly value.

Max

Max is the consummate entrepreneur. He spends virtually every waking hour running his company, leaving precious little for anything else; as a result, his lifestyle cost is a measly $400,000 per year.[3] His $60 billion net worth is so far above his Number that the whole exercise of calculating the difference feels silly. However, Max has other considerations that Ben and Clare do not.

One is his legacy. While he's still a few hundred billion dollars away from being the richest man in the world, it's not out of the question that he could get there some day—his net worth has been climbing by an average of $5 billion per year for more than a decade, after all. Max doesn't speak of this ambition in public, but in his heart of hearts, it has always been his dream to hold this title.

A second consideration is that virtually his entire net worth is tied up in his company's stock. Even if he decided to embrace generosity and give most of his money away, selling a large portion of his stock would crash the share price and cause him to lose control of his company. This would obviously be unacceptable to him.

So what's the solution?

Regarding his legacy, one solution would be to switch his ambition from having the most to giving the most. If he wants to be the richest man in the world, he would need to increase his net worth by more than six times just to be in the running (and he'd still be behind Elon Musk). While such a goal is not impossible by any means, it's far from assured.

If he instead decided to divide his net worth by six—keeping $10 billion and giving away $50 billion—he would instantly become one of the most generous people in history, behind only Warren Buffett and Bill Gates. He would maintain the status of being a deca-billionaire, and even a modest return on that $10 billion would cover his

3. This does not include the cost of his private jet, which he uses almost exclusively for work, or security, both of which are covered by his company. Such expenses are customary for high-profile businesspeople, and so it makes sense to think of them as business rather than personal expenses.

lifestyle cost a thousand times over. Furthermore, if he earns the S&P 500 historical average return of 10%, he can give away an additional $1 billion per year and claim the title of the most generous person in history some time around his 52nd birthday.

If Max could just shift his mindset to value generosity over personal enrichment, this becomes the easiest decision in the world: why spend years chasing an uncertain lesser legacy when he can claim the guaranteed greater legacy right now?

As for keeping control of his company and maintaining its share price, he can achieve this as well, and the exact mechanism varies based on whether his company has a single- or dual-class share structure.[4] Using a single-class structure as an example, this is how he would do it: Max would transfer his shares into a voting trust, naming himself as trustee. In exchange, he gets voting trust certificates, which represent the money value of the donated shares with none of the voting rights. Max can then gradually sell these certificates over time (to avoid crashing the stock), give the money away, and retain control of his company through the trust.

The potential good that someone like Max could do for the world cannot be overstated. In addition to having a ton of money he can personally give away, his status as a deca-billionaire tech founder makes him extremely influential. It would only take one person like Max to make a move like the one described here to start a tidal wave of generosity. With more than one hundred Americans commanding a net worth over $10 billion, the only question is who will be the first to step up.

My Number

I don't remember exactly when or how it happened, but somewhere around the time I made my first million dollars in my late twenties, I decided I wanted to be worth $100 million. I settled on this amount because it felt achievable, it's a nice round number, and when I did

4. It can be done with either structure, though it's easier with dual-class.

the math I simply couldn't imagine needing any more money than this. So why bother going further?

This realization—that wealth past a certain point has no point—became the germ of an idea, which over time developed into the book you're reading now. The funny thing is that as the years passed and I gradually got closer to my goal, I began to wonder whether I had aimed too high. Did I really need that much money, and if not, should I abandon my original goal after more than a decade of effort?

This nagging doubt was heightened as I began writing this book, which not only forced me to engage in deeper introspection on this question, but also introduced new variables that have made it harder to answer. I'll walk through some of these considerations now, and you can check out Appendix B for more details on how I arrived at my Number.

Lifestyle cost: My current lifestyle is pretty modest, which is partly a function of having simple tastes and partly because I'm working and raising two small boys, leaving little time for leisure. If I intended to live this way forever, I would already be past my Number. However, the most comfortable lifestyle I would realistically want to live—which includes a much larger primary residence, a vacation home, frequent and luxurious travel, and some expensive hobbies—would cost more. To pay for it, I would need a higher net worth than I have now, but not quite $100 million.

Sources of wealth: My net worth is similar to Ben's, but with one major difference: a large chunk of it is illiquid and difficult to precisely value. Depending on the value of these assets, my net worth may be a bit higher or a bit lower than I think it is. To account for this, I'm estimating conservatively and planning for scenarios where my true net worth may be substantially lower than it is on paper.

Building AboveWealth.org: Writing this book prompted me to recalculate my Number for the first time in years and see that my ideal lifestyle costs less than $100 million. It also inspired me to start AboveWealth.org, which will require substantial investment if the ideas in this book catch on. Eventually, I plan to make the platform self-sustaining via a combination of small transaction fees and direct support from donors, but until then I will be funding it myself. Therefore, I'm earmarking $10 million of my net worth for this purpose.

Putting all of this together: As you can see in Appendix B, my revised Number is $90 million. When I account for my ideal lifestyle and a comfortable buffer, I can't imagine needing more than this. With that said, I'm going to revisit this exercise about once a year to see if I should raise or lower it. In addition to the $90 million for myself and my family, I'm building in a buffer of up to $10 million to invest in AboveWealth.org. This means I'm going to continue pushing toward my original Number of $100 million for now, but will likely reduce my Number to $90 million in the future.

5

THE PROBLEMS GENEROSITY COULD SOLVE

"If you set a crazy, ambitious goal and miss it, you'll still achieve something remarkable."
— Larry Page

Perhaps the single greatest enabling factor for the ultra wealthy endlessly maximizing their net worth is that virtually no one expects them to do otherwise. It's mind-boggling how rarely this is acknowledged, and in fact as I write this sentence, I'm fairly certain I've never heard anyone point out this obvious yet extremely powerful fact. But just imagine the opposite—a society where capping your wealth at a reasonable level is an expectation on par with respecting one's elders or telling the truth. Anyone amassing tens or hundreds of billions of dollars in such a society would be the object of constant scorn. In our society, we put them on the Forbes 400 with an airbrushed headshot and a glowing bio.

Expectations matter. Even the people who despise the ultra wealthy and think billionaires shouldn't exist don't frame their criticism as disappointment or an expectation that the wealthy would act any differently than they currently do. For them, billionaires are like a bear who wanders into your campsite: a threat and something to be dealt with, certainly, but not something you can reason with or blame for wanting to eat you. A bear is just gonna bear. Similarly, most people treat it as a fait accompli that billionaires are gonna billionaire and go on amassing wealth.

The difference between me and these people is that I don't think of billionaires as a force of nature or a mindless animal. They're just people. Most have never asked themselves why they continue to amass wealth, and unless society puts some onus on them to do so, most of them never will. That doesn't mean they're evil or can't be reached. Many of us are guilty of doing bad things for no other reason than the fact that we haven't really thought about it. For example, littering was commonplace before years of PSAs and pressure from environmental groups mostly stamped it out. Were all those litterbugs bad people? No, they just never really thought about what they were doing.

If more people thought deeply about this topic, I think our society would change for the better. I often wonder how the average person would feel if they understood A) just how much excess money the ultra wealthy have, and B) how much better the world would be if they gave that money away. Would we still expect people to endlessly amass wealth, or would we start asking why they're not putting that money to better use?

How much excess wealth is there in the world?

Open your favorite finance or economics textbook and look up the term **excess wealth.** You won't find it because I just made it up, a fact that has some pluses and minuses. In the positive column it means I can define it however I want. In the negative, I can already hear a certain subset of readers grumbling about how I can't make a "real" point based on an economic concept I just invented.

With apologies to the pedants, I'm going to define excess wealth as net worth beyond one's Number. It's the net worth you don't need, won't spend, and is just there for bragging rights. It's the money that would be much better utilized solving the world's problems.

So how much of it is there?

This is a tricky question to answer, and one that requires some assumptions and judgment calls. Let's start by saying that only centi-millionaires and above possess any excess wealth. While this is absolutely not the case—plenty of deca-millionaires have net worths above their Number—it's helpful to draw the line here for two reasons. First, we can safely assume almost everyone with a net worth north of $100 million has at least some excess wealth, which simplifies the math and saves us from having to figure out which deca-millionaires have excess wealth and which don't. Second, when someone inevitably claims that I'm exaggerating how much excess wealth there is in the world, I can counter by saying that my estimate is so conservative, it assumes a grand total of $0 coming from the world's 2.3 million deca-millionaires.[1]

Let's make a couple more assumptions. Back in the preface, I described the lifestyle that $1 billion can buy: $200 million in homes around the world, a $100 million mega-yacht, $50 million for a private jet, $50 million for collectibles like art and cars, and $600 million invested generating over $50 million per year—enough to spend nearly $140,000 every single day. For the sake of argument, I'm going to say this is all anyone really needs, and that net worth beyond $1 billion is, by definition, excess wealth.[2] Therefore, in this thought experiment, I'm going to imagine that every billionaire in the world gives away all of their net worth beyond $1 billion.

In a similar vein, I'm going to assume all centi-millionaires scale down to $100 million. This is a more aggressive and less defensible assumption, given that there are many centi-millionaires who actu-

---

1. https://link.cnbc.com/public/38877848
2. I can only imagine how many monocles are falling into teacups at the idea of only needing $1 billion to be happy. I have to admit the number sounds low to me as well, but I think that's a function of how desensitized we are to eye-popping net worth. When you actually add up all the things you can buy with $1 billion, as I've done here, it sure does seem like more than enough, doesn't it?

couldn't fund their current lifestyle with only $100 million. Remember, though, that I'm leaving deca-millionaires out of this entirely; including even the most conservative estimate of that group's excess wealth would more than offset a slight overestimation of the excess wealth held by centi-millionaires.

Okay, so where does this leave us?

There are about 3,000 billionaires in the world, with a collective net worth of $16 trillion.[3] Numbers for centi-millionaires are harder to come by as there are far more of them and they're not tracked as closely, but the best estimate puts the total number at about 30,000 people.[4] If we assume their net worth is evenly distributed across the $100 million–$1 billion range, that puts the average net worth at $550 million, or $16.5 trillion for the whole cohort.

If every billionaire scales down to $1 billion, that leaves $13 trillion in excess wealth; for the centi-millionaires scaling down to $100 million, that's an additional $13.5 trillion in excess wealth, for a total of $26.5 trillion. If the average deca-millionaire chipped in just $1.5 million it would bring the total to $30 trillion, but we're leaving them out and I prefer to be conservative so let's round down to $25 trillion.

What could we do with $25 trillion?

Before we proceed to what could be accomplished with $25 trillion, let's first establish a framework for prioritizing the things we could spend that money on. One approach would be to identify the various needs that all human beings have and see how many of them we can satisfy for the greatest number of people, starting with the most fundamental needs.

The American psychologist Abraham Maslow famously proposed his "hierarchy of needs" in 1943. While this theory has largely fallen out of favor—mostly due to its subjectivity and lack of empirical

---

3. https://fortune.com/2025/04/02/world-record-number-of-billionaires-wealth-higher-than-most-gdp-despite-stock-market-bloodbath/

4. https://www.henleyglobal.com/publications/centi-millionaire-report-2024

evidence—the fundamental needs it identifies are still widely known and accepted. The most basic needs in the hierarchy are the physiological requirements for survival: water, air, food, shelter, clothing, reproduction, and sleep. Then comes safety: personal safety, financial security, and health.

But wait, there's a snag. For certain issues, the problem has less to do with money than conditions on the ground. Malnutrition in Africa is a good example. It's fairly straightforward to calculate the number of people who need food assistance, multiply by the per person cost to feed them, and arrive at a number. But this doesn't account for the fact that in the real world, much of this assistance is likely to end up in the hands of warlords and corrupt politicians. It's both inaccurate and naive to put a price tag on solving world hunger without accounting for this.

In my research for this book, many people cited this fact in order to shut down the conversation.

Question: what does it cost to solve world hunger?

Answer: it doesn't matter because warlords will just hijack whatever aid you provide.

This is a pretty unsatisfying answer. While the point is valid, it doesn't change the fact that there are hundreds of millions of malnourished people in the world, and theoretically we should be able to address that (and money will definitely help).

To square this circle, I'm going to do two different versions of this exercise. The first will look at the United States, focusing exclusively on domestic issues that could be solved by greater generosity. While the US isn't exactly corruption-free, we don't have roaming militias to worry about (yet!), and so it's safe to assume most of this money will end up where it's supposed to.

The second version will be global, and so will be impacted by challenges like the one cited above. Because there are so many more extraneous factors here, I'm not going to go into this version in anywhere near as much depth, as the risk of proposing unrealistic solutions is just too high. Instead, I will present some ideas to solve a handful of important problems, and I'll leave plenty of wiggle room in the budget to account for the more challenging environment. Given how many global problems are impossible to tackle without military or diplomatic intervention, this seems like a good compromise.

My hope is that this approach will satisfy two separate camps. One group of people looks at conversations around inequality and feels they are too first-world centric. They ask why we're so focused on Americans being able to afford a larger house when there are millions of people in the world dying of disease and hunger; these people will presumably be more aligned with the global approach. Another group makes the fair point that the world is a messed up place and it's not America's job to solve everyone's problems, so we should take care of our own first—especially given the added challenge of helping people in corrupt and war-torn places. For them, the America-centric approach will be more resonant.

$12.5 trillion to solve America's problems

Can the excess wealth of the world's richest people ensure that basic needs are met for all 350 million people living in the United States? Before we answer that, we should acknowledge that foreign centi-millionaires and billionaires are unlikely to give their excess wealth to the richest country in history, and so we need to scale this down to the amount controlled by Americans. This data is not available, but from my research it seems that 40–50% is a reasonable estimate—I'm going to go with 50%, i.e. $12.5 trillion. This amount invested in an endowment earning an 8% return would fund a **$1 trillion annual budget**. Starting with the most basic needs, let's work our way up and see how far we get.

WATER: Most of us consider this problem pretty well solved in the US, but the Environmental Protection Agency (EPA) estimates that up to 9 million homes are served through legacy lead pipes across the country; there is no safe level of lead exposure, and the list of harms it can cause is long.[5] According to estimates from the EPA and the Brookings Institution, there are about 4 million lead service lines nationwide, and it would cost an average of $4,700 per line to replace them, for a total **one-time cost of $18.8 billion.**[6] The Environmental Defense Fund estimates that each full lead service line replaced would yield $22,000 in economic benefits from reduced cardiovascular disease mortality alone, a Return on Investment (ROI) of 368%.[7]

AIR: Like water, air is something that most of us take for granted, despite the fact that 46% of Americans, 156.1 million people, live in places with failing grades for unhealthy levels of ozone or particle pollution.[8] Air pollution is responsible for about 100,000 deaths per year in the US, and while estimates of economic cost vary, multiple sources put it in the range of $700–$800 billion per year.[9]

Unlike water, there are many initiatives we would need to tackle to fully solve the problem, and the full price tag would run into the trillions of dollars per year. The situation is further complicated by the fact that the EPA estimates that every dollar invested in clean air returns between $30 and $90 in health and economic benefits.[10] If we split the difference and say the real number is $60, and if we assume some clever entrepreneur could figure out how to capture even 5% of that economic upside for himself, then he'd make $3 for every $1

5. In children, it can cause reduced IQ, language development, and attention span, and increased aggression and impulsivity. Prolonged exposure for both children and adults can damage the brain and nervous system, reduce fertility, and increase the risk of high blood pressure, heart disease, kidney disease, and cancer.

6. https://www.epa.gov/newsreleases/epa-announces-3-billion-new-funding-states-reduce-lead-drinking-water; https://www.brookings.edu/articles/what-would-it-cost-to-replace-all-the-nations-lead-water-pipes/

7. https://www.edf.org/media/mayors-roadmap-paving-way-healthier-cities

8. https://www.lung.org/research/sota/key-findings

9. https://pubs.acs.org/doi/10.1021/acs.estlett.0c00424; https://www.nrdc.org/sites/default/files/costs-inaction-burden-health-report.pdf; https://www.state.gov/key-topics-office-of-environmental-quality-and-transboundary-issues/air-quality/

10. https://www.epa.gov/clean-air-act-overview/benefits-and-costs-clean-air-act-1990-2020-second-prospective-study

invested, with the remaining $57 in positive externalities going to all of us.

This begs the question as to why some billionaire hasn't already made this his pet project, making billions in profits, saving tens of thousands of lives per year, and covering himself in glory in the process. Or maybe some billionaire already has? After all, what is the value proposition of electric cars if not reducing emissions, and isn't that how the richest person in the world made most of his money? How are other billionaires not piling into clean air projects? But I digress...

Just to bite off a little chunk of this problem for the purpose of this exercise, here are two cheap and easy things we could do. For a **one-time cost of $40 billion**, we could replace 10 million old wood stoves with cleaner burning EPA-certified ones, saving 10,000 lives per year and generating an annual economic benefit of $56–$126 billion.[11] For **$15 billion per year**, we could subsidize manure injection and cover storage lagoons to cut ammonia emissions by 50%, saving 20,000 lives per year and generating hundreds of billions of dollars per year in economic benefits.[12]

FOOD: The federal Supplemental Nutrition Assistance Program (SNAP) program costs American taxpayers about $100 billion per year and provides benefits to 42 million people. Experts estimate the full cost to end food insecurity in the US is an additional $25 billion per year.[13] A conservative estimate of the annual healthcare costs attributable to hunger and food insecurity put the figure at around

11. https://www.epa.gov/burnwise/implementing-wood-burning-changeout-campaigns-and-examples-programs; https://www.angi.com/articles/wood-burning-stove-installation-cost.htm; https://www.tandfonline.com/doi/full/10.1080/10962247.2025.2488807#abstract; https://www.epa.gov/sites/default/files/2016-11/documents/kit_2_fast_facts.pdf

12. https://pubs.acs.org/doi/10.1021/es060379a; https://sustainability.stanford.edu/news/identifying-sources-deadly-air-pollution-us; https://www.sciencedirect.com/science/article/abs/pii/S0048969717334836

13. https://www.globalgiving.org/learn/how-much-would-it-cost-to-end-world-hunger

$160 billion.[14] Therefore, if we use **$125 billion per year** of our budget to address food insecurity: millions of Americans would be healthier and save $160 billion on healthcare costs; we could eliminate SNAP completely and reduce the federal budget deficit by $100 billion; and, millions of low-income people wouldn't have to work multiple jobs just to put food on the table.

SHELTER: This is the big one. When we talk about the affordability crisis in America, we're mostly talking about housing. It's the same thing when it comes to Gen Z's loss of faith in capitalism and the American Dream—their parents had a realistic path to building wealth through home ownership, and they don't. The US has a housing deficit of 3–7 million units, and experts agree that both supply and demand side interventions are needed to close the gap (mostly supply).

If we spent $145 billion per year on the supply side, we could: subsidize the creation and preservation of more than 350,000 units annually for households earning less than 50% of the Area Median Income (AMI); provide grants for zoning reform to unlock millions of new market-rate units that lower overall prices; invest in prefabricated construction and land acquisition to lower per-unit construction costs; compensate landlords for dedicating a percentage of units to households earning less than 80% of AMI.

For $90 billion per year on the demand side, we could end evictions by fully funding universal housing vouchers for extremely low-income households, and provide housing and on-site services for every chronically homeless person in the US. Housing the homeless would not only be a huge quality of life improvement for everyone (not just the homeless), it would actually generate a net savings, since the associated costs of homelessness such as emergency services, jail, and healthcare exceed the cost of housing them.

And finally, for $35 billion, we could fund a down payment

14. https://www.hungerreport.org/costofhunger/

assistance program that would provide $25,000 grants to 1.4 million first-time home buyers every year. Such a program would help millions of people get on the housing ladder and start to build their own wealth and financial security through home ownership, just as previous generations did.

This total investment of **$270 billion per year** would create a huge economic stimulus: hundreds of thousands of new jobs, better wages and labor mobility, reduced stress and improved mental health, increased productivity, local government savings from reduced homelessness, and more. See Appendix C for a detailed budget breakdown and sources.

Clothing: While clothing is indeed one of our most basic needs, the United States actually has a huge surplus of it, and even the poorest Americans can get clothing for free. In fact, the US has so much more clothing than we need that we're the world's #1 exporter of used clothing—about 750,000 tons annually, which makes up 40% of the global market.[15] Nothing needed here!

Reproduction: Birth rates have been declining across the developed world for decades, and the United States is no exception. This demographic crunch presents a serious risk to future stability, as a society with too many seniors and not enough working people simply cannot function. One of the biggest drivers of our declining birth rate is affordability.[16] Millions of Americans cannot afford maternity costs, childcare, and basic necessities.

President Joe Biden's Build Back Better Act (BBB) originally included $20 billion per year for a paid family and medical leave

15. https://greenamerica.org/unraveling-fashion-industry/what-really-happens-unwanted-clothes; https://www.usda.gov/about-usda/news/blog/exporting-used-textiles-helps-global-and-local-economies

16. https://www.unfpa.org/press/unfpa-report-links-falling-birth-rates-cost-living-sexist-norms-fear-future

program. This program would have covered nearly all US workers, and provided a minimum of four weeks of paid leave for the birth or placement of a child, or to care for oneself or a family member in the event of a serious medical condition.[17] An additional $5 billion per year would be enough to cover necessities like formula, diapers, cribs, and car seats for those who can't afford it.[18]

Next comes childcare, which is a bigger cost. Multiple policy analyses estimate that nationwide universal childcare from birth through age five would cost about $140 billion annually.[19]

Adding all of this up, we could address this issue for **$165 billion per year.**

Sleep: Look at virtually any ranking of the reasons people struggle with sleep, and you'll see that many of them tie directly to lack of income and resources. Stress is a huge one, particularly when it relates to finances, health, and caregiving. Untreated health conditions like sleep apnea, chronic pain, and GERD are another major factor. Lack of physical activity, often a result of simply not having time to exercise, also ranks high. All of these things would be helped immensely by addressing the other things on this list. While it's possible that we may want to allocate resources to specifically address sleep at some point in the future, for the purposes of this exercise I'm going to say that better sleep is free with the price of admission here.

Personal Safety: This is another one that's hard to put a price tag on. The top three threats to Americans' personal safety are car

17. https://www.cbo.gov/publication/57631
18. https://nationaldiaperbanknetwork.org/wp-content/uploads/2022/12/NDBN_DiaperNeed_Overview_Dec_2022-.pdf
https://www.whattoexpect.com/getting-pregnant/preparing-for-baby/work-and-finance/what-babies-really-cost.aspx
19. https://www.edweek.org/teaching-learning/how-much-would-high-quality-universal-early-care-cost-try-140-billion-a-year/2018/03

crashes, drug overdoses, and guns. It's hard to come up with something that billionaires are supposed to do about traffic accidents, and gun control is a famously intractable political problem, not an economic one. Large cities spend millions of dollars per year fighting drug overdoses, but that only goes so far given how hard it is to get at the root causes of addiction.

Like sleep, personal safety is another area where addressing the other problems on this list, particularly housing, likely puts a big dent in the problem. Revitalizing failing neighborhoods and providing better job opportunities would cut into the gang violence that drives so many gun deaths. Affordable housing and better programs to stop people from falling into homelessness would cut down on overdoses and other harms that come from living on the street. Ultimately, no amount of money will ever make a society perfectly safe, but it seems clear that addressing the other needs on this list would have an ancillary benefit of making America safer.

HEALTH: Policy experts have been debating how to fix America's broken healthcare system for decades, and I won't pretend that I can offer anything like a solution in a couple paragraphs here. It makes no sense to waste a large chunk of our $1 trillion budget on healthcare when we know costs are much higher than they ought to be; before throwing money at this problem, we need to first address the causes of these inflated prices, which is outside the scope of this exercise.

Instead of trying to fix a giant, complex, and thoroughly broken system, I propose biting off one little chunk of it. Medical emergencies are the leading cause of bankruptcy in the United States, with 67% of bankruptcies citing medical expenses as a contributor.[20] Of the approximately $505 billion that Americans pay out of pocket on healthcare each year, 46% comes from the top 5% of spenders; these are the people facing catastrophic costs that can lead to financial ruin

20. https://pmc.ncbi.nlm.nih.gov/articles/PMC6366487/

and bankruptcy. Doing the math, it would therefore cost about **$232 billion per year** to cover these costs and reduce, if not entirely end, medical bankruptcy.[21]

Financial Security: In the last section, we pivoted away from the intractable problem of fixing the entire healthcare system and instead addressed the more manageable problem of medical bankruptcy, which is actually the single largest threat to financial security in the United States. Another important part of achieving financial security is a high-paying job, and for that we need to develop our workforce.

The United States has a severe shortage of electricians, plumbers, HVAC techs, welders, and carpenters. For $100 billion annually, we could: fund 1.5 million paid apprenticeships at $40,000 per year for both young people entering the workforce and older workers who need retraining; cover $15,000 in tuition, equipment, and tools for 1.67 million vocational students; support the above programs with $15 billion per year in employer incentives and job placement.

For $53 billion per year, we could provide $3,000 in tuition assistance to 10.9 million community college students, and $7,500 to an additional 2.7 million students to cover certificate programs in healthcare, IT, and manufacturing.

For $40 billion per year, we could provide $5,000 per year in living expense assistance to 8 million vocational and community college students.

The total cost for all of this is **$193 billion per year.**

Summing up: Excluding the one-time costs of $18.8 billion and $40

---

21. https://www.cms.gov/data-research/statistics-trends-and-reports/national-health-expenditure-data/nhe-fact-sheet; https://www.commonwealthfund.org/publications/issue-briefs/2020/apr/catastrophic-out-of-pocket-costs-problem-middle-income

billion to address acute water and air issues, respectively, the programs I've listed here come out to $1 trillion per year exactly.

- Air: $15 billion
- Food: $125 billion
- Shelter: $270 billion
- Reproduction: $165 billion
- Health: $232 billion
- Financial Security: $193 billion
- Sleep and Personal Safety: Free

If you go through a list of what ails America, you'll find that many of our most pervasive problems are largely or entirely solved by the items in this budget. Here are just some of the benefits we would receive.

- Protect children from brain damage and adults from heart disease by eliminating lead from our water supply.
- Save 30,000 lives per year and improve the health of millions of others by reducing air pollution.
- End food insecurity, eliminate SNAP, and reduce the federal deficit by $100 billion.
- Build 350,000 homes per year, reduce housing costs, help millions of people afford a down payment, and end evictions and homelessness.[22]
- Provide universal paid family and medical leave, as well as universal childcare through age five.
- Improve people's sleep and mental health by alleviating financial, health, and caregiving stress.
- Make our communities safer by reducing gang violence and addressing homelessness.

22. Yes, some homeless people would still choose to live on the street, but at least there would be guaranteed money to house anyone who wants to be housed.

- End, or at least vastly reduce, the #1 cause of financial ruin (medical bankruptcy).
- Close the skilled labor gap, create millions of high-paying jobs, and either fully or mostly cover the cost of community college and vocational training for tens of millions of students.

Addressing these problems would be nothing short of transformational for the American people. And when you consider that most of these things produce positive externalities that significantly exceed their cost, it's safe to assume we'd see a massive boost to the economy as yet another benefit.

Now, do I expect everyone with a net worth over $100 million to give enough to cover all of this? No, not in the short term, though in the long term anything is possible. But that's beside the point. The purpose of this exercise is to simply do a back-of-the-envelope calculation of how much *excess* wealth these **16,500** people have—meaning they don't need it and will never spend it—and how much better off **350,000,000** people would be if they gave it away. I have to imagine that if the average American was aware of this, they would start asking what these enormous fortunes are being used for that's more worthy than this. I also think a meaningful percentage of wealthy people—by no means all, but more than just a few—would say, "You know what? My life would be exactly the same if I had $1 billion instead of $10 billion, and I want to help."

$25 trillion to solve the world's problems

That's the American picture, now let's zoom out and look at the global landscape. As stated above, I'm not going to do this analysis in as much detail because there are just so many extraneous factors and unknowns when we're talking about solving global problems. The framework I used for the US exercise was to see how many of our most basic needs could be met with $1 trillion per year (turns out it's quite a lot!). For the global exercise, I'm going to use a $2 trillion annual budget and limit my focus to just three things: ending extreme global poverty, ending hunger, and substantially ending deaths from infectious diseases.

Let's start with ending extreme global poverty. Paul Niehaus—one of the founders of GiveDirectly, a non-profit that provides direct cash transfers to people living in extreme poverty—shared some salient facts in a recent TED Talk. He pointed out that between 1980 and 2020, the share of the global population living in extreme poverty declined from 44% to 9%.[23] He also cited a Brookings estimate that the remaining poverty gap, i.e. the cost to bring that last 9% out of extreme poverty, is **$100 billion per year.**[24]

I have two reactions to this. First, his point about the decline of global poverty since 1980 should be interpreted as hopeful evidence that big problems, which often feel so intractable, actually can be solved. It should *not* be used as a talking point to dispel the seriousness of wealth inequality. I can imagine someone on the other side of this debate saying, "If we've made all this progress on global poverty, how can you say wealth inequality is a growing problem?" The answer is that wealth inequality in the developed world and global poverty in the developing world are two separate issues; it's entirely possible for one to worsen while the other improves.

My second takeaway is that $100 billion is only 5% of the $2 trillion in annual income our theoretical endowment would generate. That's a drop in the bucket, and it makes me think we should aim higher. If the cost to end extreme poverty is only $100 billion, I would argue this is the absolute minimum the world's ultra wealthy should aspire to, and that we should identify some higher standard to bring these people to and aim for that.

Moving onto hunger, let's first point out that ending extreme poverty goes a long way toward solving this problem. Almost all people facing chronic hunger are also living in poverty, and so by

---

23. https://www.youtube.com/watch?v=vrQwahPQ6YI

24. https://www.brookings.edu/articles/a-purpose-driven-fund-to-end-extreme-poverty-by-2030/

giving these people cash to lift them out of poverty, we're also giving them purchasing power to buy food. However, there is still an additional cost that would need to be paid to end hunger. This is because there are other drivers of hunger beyond just poverty, such as famine, war, and outdated infrastructure that's vulnerable to climate risks and spoilage. The UN World Food Programme estimates that **$93 billion per year** is needed to achieve their goal of ending world hunger by 2030, with the funds being used for emergency aid, agricultural research, climate-resilient farming, and infrastructure.[25]

Finally, we turn to the world's most deadly infectious diseases, which are tuberculosis, AIDS, and malaria. Combined, these three diseases kill about 2.4 million people per year. Getting a definitive estimate of the cost to end these epidemics is difficult, largely because so much of the research is aimed at identifying the highest ROI ways to reduce the most deaths for the least amount of money. (A quick digression: the fact that it's relatively easy to find data on the cost to substantially reduce deaths but difficult to find data on ending them is a sad reflection of the state of global generosity, as it suggests the researchers don't expect anyone to foot the whole bill and so don't even bother answering the question—hopefully this is something we can change.) Piecing together data from The Global Fund and the UN, **$50 billion per year** appears to be a defensible estimate of the cost to end these epidemics, either substantially or completely.[26]

Putting this together: $100 billion for poverty, $100 billion for hunger (rounding up from $93 billion), and $50 billion for disease adds up to **$250 billion per year**, a mere 12.5% of our overall budget. You can look at this in two ways, and both are encouraging.

If you think a $2 trillion budget is feasible, that means we'd have $1.75 trillion left over for the kinds of things outlined in the American exercise above. Health, housing, education, and financial security

25. https://news.un.org/en/story/2025/11/1166397
26. http://theglobalfund.org/en/investment-case/; https://www.who.int/teams/global-programme-on-tuberculosis-and-lung-health/tb-reports/global-tuberculosis-report-2023/financing-for-tb-prevention--diagnostic-and-treatment-services

could all be massively improved if the global equation is anything like the US.

If you think a $2 trillion budget is unrealistic, the lesson here is that we don't need that much. At an 8% annual return, the world's wealthiest people would only need to give away a little over $3 trillion —not the $25 trillion used for this exercise—to generate the $250 billion per year needed to solve these problems. Put another way, if you think my estimate of global excess wealth is too aggressive, that's fine because we'd need less than 15% of it to address global poverty, hunger, and disease.

While most of this book focuses on the messaging and tactics we should use to influence people in the developed world, we shouldn't lose sight of the reasons for doing all of this. There's a world of good the ultra wealthy could do, if they only had the will.

I'M NOT A POLICY EXPERT, and I fully acknowledge that a lot of work would need to be done to get the details right before enacting these proposals. With that said, my argument doesn't depend on plus or minus X%. Say I'm underestimating some of these costs, and what I've proposed here only solves 60% of the problem: great, we solved 60% of the problem! Or say I'm overestimating: great, it costs less than we thought!

In researching this chapter, it was disappointing how many people tried to dismiss the entire premise as naive. I understand perfectly well that what I'm describing here is how I think the world should be, and not how it is, but that doesn't mean we shouldn't try. To all the naysayers, all I can do is quote Google co-founder Larry Page: "If you set a crazy, ambitious goal and miss it, you'll still achieve something remarkable."

Yeah, let's do that.

6

HOW NOT TO SOLVE THIS PROBLEM

"Billionaires shouldn't exist."
— The Internet

Conversations about wealth inequality are everywhere these days. Turn on the TV, listen to a podcast, or go on social media, and it won't be long before it comes up. Everyone is aware of the problem and most agree that action is needed, so one would think something would get done to fix it. But nothing ever does. Why?

I think it's because conventional wisdom on this topic has been hijacked by a monomaniacal focus on government action and taxes; advocates doggedly push the same proposals year after year, unfazed by decades of failure. To see this groupthink for yourself, try asking the three leading AI models (ChatGPT, Claude, and Google Gemini) the same question: what are the top five most commonly proposed solutions for reducing wealth inequality? While their answers differ to some degree, every single proposal is a government intervention and about half are around tax policy.

ChatGPT: raise taxes on the wealthy; raise minimum wage; expand safety net programs; Universal Basic Income (UBI); break up big tech / monopolies.

Claude: progressive wealth tax; higher marginal income tax; increased capital gains tax; stronger antitrust enforcement; UBI or expanded social programs.

Gemini: wealth tax; raise minimum wage; expand tax credits for the working poor; increase the top marginal income tax rate; student loan forgiveness.

So I guess we have our answer, right? This is a problem for the government to solve. I'm sure they'll get right on it once they've ended the latest self-imposed shutdown, overturned *Citizens United*, and figured out which bathrooms we should all be using.[1] It's remarkable how many people can correctly diagnose the ills of wealth inequality in one breath, and then in the next propose a series of government interventions that assume we have a competent Congress that's not bought and paid for by the wealthy. We don't have that, and even if we did these proposals wouldn't be the best way to solve the problem.

The question is not whether getting billionaires to pay their fair share of taxes would reduce wealth inequality, because of course it would. The question is whether we're getting any closer to achieving that goal, and the answer to this is also obvious: we're not. To understand why, we need to have an honest conversation about the many issues with taxes as a solution to wealth inequality. When we do, it becomes clear that tax policy on its own is doomed to fail. It must be paired with persuasion.

We can't tax our way out of wealth inequality

The ultra wealthy generally don't want to pay higher taxes, and by

---

1. *Citizens United v. Federal Election Commission* was a 2010 Supreme Court decision that ruled that corporations can spend unlimited money on independent political broadcasts and ads. It's commonly cited as the primary driver for the outsize influence that wealthy interests have over the government, including on tax policy.

definition have more resources than anyone else to fight higher taxes and shield their wealth from the IRS. Do you know who would have to reform the tax code? Politicians. Do you know who owns politicians? Rich people. Even if we could overcome billions of dollars' worth of lobbying and other influence, we'd still be left with sophisticated tax evasion schemes and expensive enforcement. Congress can barely tie its shoes, but for some reason we think they can tackle this?

Then there's the question of who we're taxing and how much. High-income blue state residents already pay around 50% of their income in federal, state, and local taxes—the same as Denmark. Meanwhile, thanks to legal tax avoidance, America's wealthiest pay just 3.4% when their wealth growth is counted as income, and only 15.8% on their reported taxable income.[2] It is completely indefensible to tell someone making seven figures that the 50% they're already paying isn't enough, when people with a net worth 1,000 times higher are paying close to zero. If we're going to talk about raising taxes, we need to figure out how to get billionaires to pay anything like their fair share before raising taxes on the working wealthy by a single cent.

So how do we do that? In theory, a wealth tax is the answer; in practice, they haven't worked. Unlike income from wages, which is easy for the IRS to track and tax, wealth and the income it generates present a much greater challenge. In 1990, twelve European countries had wealth taxes; today, only three still do.[3] The other nine repealed them due to implementation issues, capital flight, a failure to raise projected revenues, and the cost of enforcement often exceeding the benefits. This makes the political challenge of a wealth tax even greater than other forms of taxation. Not only would we need a plan that addresses the reasons it failed in Europe, the fact of that failure provides powerful ammunition for the army of lobbyists who would

2. https://www.propublica.org/article/the-secret-irs-files-trove-of-never-before-seen-records-reveal-how-the-wealthiest-avoid-income-tax; https://www.propublica.org/article/you-may-be-paying-a-higher-tax-rate-than-a-billionaire

3. https://www.npr.org/sections/money/2019/02/26/698057356/if-a-wealth-tax-is-such-a-good-idea-why-did-europe-kill-theirs

try to defeat it—why are we enacting a policy that had to be repealed in 75% of the countries that tried it? Assuming the bill's proponents could answer that question well enough to get it passed, we'd still face difficult and expensive enforcement that would eat into the revenues raised.

What about corporate taxes? You may be surprised to learn that the United States actually had the fourth highest corporate tax rate in the world before we lowered it in 2017; today, our total combined state and federal tax rate is roughly in line with other Organization for Economic Co-operation and Development (OECD) countries.[4] Given this fact, it's hard to understand why so many progressive politicians have said it's too low and called for raising it back to the old rate of 35%. Whether they're ignorant of the facts (unlikely) or simply pandering to their constituents (more likely), such statements mislead the public and needlessly erode credibility. Their opponents get an easy talking point to dismiss legitimate progressive concerns, and the rest of us are left wondering what else these politicians are getting wrong if they can't get their facts straight on something as simple as this.

The issue is not, and never has been, the tax rate; it's the enforcement. We could raise it to 90% and it wouldn't make a bit of difference as long as corporations can use offshore shell companies and other loopholes to avoid it entirely. The solution here is obvious: set the corporate rate at a reasonable level—the current 21% is fine—and then *actually enforce it*. Make them pay it. It's no secret what these companies make in profits; apply the tax to that amount. But again, if the so-called champions of tax reform can't even get the diagnosis right—fixating on rates instead of enforcement—we cannot rely on them for the cure.

We should pause here and point out that everything covered so far is about raising tax revenues, not addressing inequality. Part of the monomania around solving wealth inequality with taxes is that no

---

4. https://taxpolicycenter.org/briefing-book/how-do-us-corporate-income-tax-rates-and-revenues-compare-other-countries

one seems to notice that they're conflating two separate issues. Reducing the deficit through some combination of higher taxes and lower spending is a good move and would help to reduce inequality, but it's not a silver bullet for two reasons. First, it does nothing to address the primary driver of wealth inequality, which I argued in Chapter 2 is the shift from a labor-intensive old economy to a software-dominated, billionaire-minting new economy. Addressing this structural shift would require solutions far more targeted and radical than the blunt tool of tax policy can provide, and in a political climate where even modest tax increases are met with fierce resistance, there is no realistic path to enacting them.

The second reason is that only about 20% of the federal budget goes toward programs that address wealth inequality, such as Medicaid, SNAP, child tax credits, education, and housing assistance. More than 50% goes to interest on our national debt, the military, Social Security, and Medicare. While some might argue Social Security and Medicare address inequality, these programs provide essentially the same benefits to all Americans regardless of income, making their impact on the problem indirect at best. We also shouldn't forget that 10% of the budget goes to Medicaid, which falls prey to the waste of our bloated and inefficient healthcare system. Putting all of this together, the argument for addressing wealth inequality with taxes is essentially this: let's allocate 20% of the money we take in to address the problem, and of that amount let's spend half on a program where a significant portion gets eaten up by improper payments, administrative costs, insurance company profits, and the generally inflated cost of healthcare.

Putting aside all the practical reasons that taxes alone won't solve inequality, there's a philosophical argument that really puts the final nail in the coffin, and it's this: if you force someone to do the right thing, you can only count on them doing it for as long as you continue to force them. If you *persuade* someone to do the right thing, you can count on them to do it on their own. Taxes are force. Without persuasion, the wealthy will evade higher taxes today and overturn them tomorrow. To solve wealth inequality in a durable way, we need to make wealthy people want to solve it.

I want to be very clear that I am *not* defending our current tax policies, and I do think tax reform is needed. If I could wave a magic wand and fix the tax code, I would drastically simplify it, enforce corporate taxes, and close the loopholes that allow the wealthiest people to underpay. I'm also a supporter of pragmatic tax policies that laser-target the ultra wealthy without penalizing people who are already paying a lot, such as New York City's tax on second homes and various proposals to close the "buy, borrow, die" loophole by taxing margin loans.

But here's the thing: there is no magic wand. There are many who will pound the table and insist that the only solution to wealth inequality is to tax the wealthy—and in their defense, it's absolutely true that most billionaires drastically underpay—but I've never heard a good explanation for how they propose to do that. I've raised several issues with taxation as a solution to inequality in this chapter, but honestly I could have stopped at the first: the wealthy don't want to pay more, and no one has figured out a way around that. If we could force them, we'd have done it by now.

Imagine two different approaches to addressing wealth inequality. In the first, you're trying to push through aggressive tax reform with politicians as your ally and billionaires as your enemy. You're relying on politicians to act in an intelligent and effective manner against billionaires, who will muster all of their immense resources to fight the politicians and hold onto as much of their wealth as possible. In the second approach, your goal is to make billionaires your ally through persuasion and avoid making enemies altogether. If this sounds naive, ask yourself whether it's any more naive than the first approach. Speaking for myself, I'd much rather have the billionaires at my side than the politicians.

More dead ends

The final chapters of this book will focus on how we make wealthy people want to address wealth inequality. But first, let's cover a few more dead ends, namely: dismissing good arguments on the other side, ignoring human nature, class warfare, and the Giving Pledge.

If all of the reasons I shared in the last section against fighting wealth inequality with taxes weren't enough, there's one more that fits better here: the sheer incompetence that runs through so much of government. Whether it's California spending tens of billions of dollars to lay zero miles of high-speed rail after nearly two decades, or the Pentagon spending $2 trillion on the F-35 fighter jet—whose strategic value would be in question at a fraction of the price—there is no shortage of examples of the government flushing our tax dollars down the toilet.

Nothing illustrates this more than the grotesque relationship between food and healthcare that our fiscal policy enables. The United States spends $3.2 billion annually on corn subsidies, which drives overproduction and artificially cheapens high-fructose corn syrup (HFCS), the primary sweetener in soda and processed foods.[5] These subsidies have contributed to a 24% decline in the price of junk food since 1985 and Americans consuming 40 pounds of HFCS per year, the highest rate in the world.[6] It's no coincidence that we're also one of the most obese countries in the world. But the real twist of the knife is that the federal government also spends over $150 billion per year treating Type 2 diabetes, a disease directly linked to excess sugar consumption, and hundreds of billions more on other conditions related to obesity. Meanwhile, less than 1% of farm subsidies are spent on fruits and vegetables.[7]

---

5. https://www.southwestledger.news/news/top-commodities-receiving-subsidies-2024
6. https://www.mountsinai.org/files/ISMMS/Assets/Media/Profiles/MS_OpEd%20Ad_Obesity_final.pdf; https://www.ebsco.com/research-starters/nutrition-and-dietetics/high-fructose-corn-syrup-hfcs
7. https://www.cdc.gov/nccdphp/priorities/diabetes-interventions.html; https://www.

Wealthy people are more likely than the average person to be aware of and repulsed by this pathological idiocy. While progressives are right to call out all the issues with our tax code, it is exceedingly rare to hear them say anything sensible about the other side of the ledger. How much of the revenue from higher taxes will actually go toward reducing inequality? Very little. Will that money be spent efficiently? No. Why is the federal government spending money to simultaneously create and solve the very same problem? Shrug.

When wealthy people *correctly* point out how poorly their tax dollars are often spent, the worst thing we can do is ignore their valid critiques and tell them they're greedy and bad, and that the only way forward is to drastically increase taxes. This approach takes any credibility and influence we might have had and lights it on fire. Instead, we need to acknowledge the limitations of government intervention, show that we've thought through potential issues, and present solutions that go beyond simply raising income tax rates. This demonstrates clear thinking about the problem rather than blind adherence to orthodoxy.

We also can't ignore human nature. I've often heard people wonder why billionaires support tax policies that are so greedy and selfish. Can't they see how wrong all of this is? No, many of them can't, and to see why, you need to understand that tax policy happens at a remove—a Grand Canyon-sized one.

Major shareholders in a large company influence a Board of Directors; the Board directs the CEO, who oversees a Public Affairs team; that team hires lawyers, accountants, and consultants, who hire lobbyists; the lobbyists cajole and bribe Congress to maintain the status quo on tax policy; that policy ultimately determines outcomes. The wealthy people driving tax policy are several degrees removed from the actual mechanism of its implementation. They will never meet one of the people their policies hurt, but they will meet regularly with highly paid yes-men whose livelihoods depend on

---

npr.org/sections/thesalt/2016/07/18/486051480/we-subsidize-crops-we-should-eat-less-of-does-this-fatten-us-up

convincing their masters that what they're doing is right and good. In their social lives, they'll rub elbows with people like them doing exactly as they are, which creates safety in numbers and fosters an "everyone else is doing it" mentality. If the ultra wealthy were forced to grapple with the consequences of their actions, many of them would likely act differently. But they aren't, so they don't.

People don't like feeling bad about themselves, and the more opportunities they have to avoid difficult introspection, the less likely it is to happen. Even the most powerful people can honestly tell themselves that they're just one person. They can't change something as byzantine and broken as the federal government, and everyone they know is acting the same way, so how bad can it be? It's much harder to deflect when the question becomes personal and the myriad obstacles to solving problems via government intervention are taken off the table. This is another reason that personalizing wealth inequality and making it a matter of persuasion will be more effective. Even the mighty Jeff Bezos can accurately say, "I don't control tax policy." But he can't say there's anything stopping him from giving tens of billions of dollars directly to the people who need it.

The next landmine to avoid is class warfare. One of the reasons the business community tends to ignore Bernie Sanders and Elizabeth Warren is that many of their positions are misguided or just plain wrong. The much larger problem, though, is they cast all wealthy people as the enemy, painting with a very broad brush that makes no distinction between a doctor with $5 million and Elon Musk with $1 trillion—we're all just "greedy millionaires and billionaires."[8] If you're trying to win someone over, the worst thing you can possibly do is cast them as the enemy, for one obvious reason: no one wants to listen to their enemy, no matter how good their arguments are. As these politicians have staked out a position that completely shuts the door on persuasion, one can only conclude that they think they can steamroll the wealthy class and get their way by force.

---

8. For the record, Bernie Sanders and Elizabeth Warren are both millionaires.

How's that working out so far, guys?

No matter how passionately we feel that we are on the right side of an argument, we can't forget that there's a difference between being right and being effective. Even if many of their points are fair, the message from these politicians creates enemies and makes billionaires *less* likely to change their behavior, since many conclude they'll be hated no matter what they do. If progressive politicians cared more about delivering results and less about virtue signaling, they'd temper their rhetoric and try to find common ground and practical solutions to the problems we face. Instead, many have spent decades demagoguing against the people they need to bring on side, rendering themselves impotent in the battle of ideas.

This brings us to the Giving Pledge, our final dead end. Launched in 2010, the pledge asks wealthy people to give away at least half their money during their lives or in their wills. Many have observed that despite its high-minded intentions, the Giving Pledge has been a flop due to lack of enforcement, wealth growth outpacing giving, and heirs reneging on the pledge. As a result, only 9 out of 256 signatories, a mere 3.5%, have actually followed through on giving away half their wealth.[9]

While I agree with the standard critiques of the Giving Pledge, I would go further and say the entire idea is backward and counterproductive. By praising billionaires for giving away their wealth after they die, the Giving Pledge implicitly endorses the idea that there is some good reason not to do it now, and that anyone needs this much money while they're living. They don't, and that message needs to be delivered forcefully if we want to have any hope of reducing wealth inequality. All the Giving Pledge does is allow billionaires to don the mantle of righteousness while continuing to maximize their net worth. As such, I think the cause of generosity would be better served by scrapping it entirely. At least then we could clearly call out the damage billionaires are doing by hoarding these jaw-dropping

9. https://fortune.com/2025/08/07/bill-gates-warren-buffett-billionaire-giving-pledge-report-wealth-inequality/

fortunes, without having the message diluted by pinky swears about giving half of it away after they die.

A true Giving Pledge would start from the assertion that no one needs tens or hundreds of billions of dollars while they're alive, and proceed from there. A pledge based on this foundation would at least have the benefit of sending the right message, and anyone signing it would be obliged to do something right now—not years or decades from now, when the trust fund brigade might decide that grandpa was off his rocker when he made all those silly promises.

TAX POLICY alone will not solve wealth inequality. Pushing higher taxes through Congress has proven nearly impossible; enforcement of wealth taxes requires high levels of cooperation from the people being taxed, and is often expensive and onerous to the point of negating the benefit; relatively little of the money will be spent addressing inequality unless we overhaul the entire federal budget; it won't address the root economic causes of rising inequality; and without changing wealthy people's minds, it will only be a matter of time until tax increases are reversed. To solve this problem, we need an approach that addresses the reasons people hoard wealth in the first place, anticipates their objections, and treats them with grace as we try to win them over to our cause.

It's time to make the case for persuasion.

7

THE CASE FOR PERSUASION

"There is only one way under high heaven to get anybody to do anything. Did you ever stop to think of that? Yes, just one way. And that is by making the other person want to do it."

— Dale Carnegie

When I tell people that I think the solution to wealth inequality is persuading rich people to be more generous, a lot of them tell me I'm nuts. Fair enough, maybe I am. But for the reasons stated in the last chapter, I think it's nuts to go all in on taxes as the answer. Thousands of politicians, NGOs, and influential people have been calling for tax reform for decades, and what do we have to show for it? The tax code is still broken and wealth inequality is only accelerating. Meanwhile, I don't hear anyone making the case for persuasion. If the definition of insanity is doing the same thing over and over again and expecting different results, it would seem that continuing to insist on taxes is insane, and trying a different approach is pretty rational.

The basis for thinking persuasion is impossible boils down to two widely held beliefs, both of which are wrong. The first is that the ultra wealthy, and billionaires in particular, are evil. I don't use that word lightly, but it's the only one that fits that frothing-at-the-mouth animus toward billionaires that you see everywhere, especially on social media. The second is that it's in billionaires' self-interest to maximize their wealth, and since they're evil they would never take the selfless action of voluntarily giving away a large portion of it.

Putting these together, the argument becomes: "You think you can persuade them? But they're evil. All they care about is money and themselves. Someone like that would never act against their self-interest. To think otherwise is so crazy it's beneath consideration."

I contend that they're not evil, it is in their self-interest to be more generous, and that persuasion is therefore possible. It's certainly worth a shot.

Why aren't the ultra wealthy more generous? Why don't we expect them to be?

The anger toward billionaires is palpable. It's also understandable. Every single day, we are reminded of the fact that there are billions of people in the world—and indeed millions in the United States, the richest country that has ever existed—either living in poverty or struggling to make ends meet. Meanwhile, a minuscule group of people possess wealth that's impossible to even conceptualize, let alone spend in a thousand lifetimes. That these blessed few could do so much for so many, sacrificing nothing in personal comfort, and yet choose not to is a great moral failing—full stop.

It's natural to look at this situation and describe billionaires in the terms we so often see. Selfish, greedy, evil. I would also use those terms to describe *this situation*, but where I get off the bus is using them to describe billionaires themselves. That's not clever hair-splitting, by the way, as this happens enough that we have a term for it: the banality of evil. The phrase was coined by German historian, journalist, and philosopher Hannah Arendt during her reporting on the 1961 trial of the Nazi Adolf Eichmann. She used the phrase to describe her observation that horrific acts can be committed by ordinary, thoughtless people just following orders or conforming to a system, rather than by sadistic monsters with deep evil intent.

That's what's happening here. When billionaires do things that seem unthinkably callous and evil to an outside observer, they're not perched in some high-backed leather chair, fingers steepled, cackling at all of us poor fools—they're trading stocks on the toilet, doomscrolling, and responding to emails. They're mechanically playing out the role our system has set for them, just as most of us are, and simply aren't thinking deeply about any of this. Part of this inattention is explained by a lack of good arguments for change, and part of it is explained by a surfeit of bad ones. When the predominant message from progressive politicians is that billionaires are a moral outrage who should not exist, it's not surprising that this audience has stopped listening.

Think about it from their perspective. Very few billionaires feel strongly enough about raising taxes that they're willing to buck their peers and make themselves a martyr for this cause. Perhaps you can fault them for that, but it's hardly unusual. There was a time when the majority of people opposed interracial marriage, the majority of businesses opposed child labor laws, the majority of men went along with denying women the vote, and so on. Ideas that seem obviously right to us today nevertheless took time and a lot of coordinated effort to catch on. Unfortunately, much of the anti-capitalist and anti-business rhetoric in the zeitgeist is so wrong, and frankly absurd, that it's easy for billionaires to dismiss their critics. Using the same broad brush that so many of us use to paint the wealthy, they could say something like, "These people are insane. They have no idea how the economy works or of the benefits that capitalism in general and my company in particular have wrought. I'm not going to listen to their nonsense about how I'm evil and shouldn't be allowed to exist."

This brings us to a crucial point. There are many times in life when there's a difference between being right and being effective, but this isn't one of them. Calling billionaires evil fails on both fronts.

For one thing, the logic of the argument wilts under the tiniest bit of scrutiny. Despite the popular caricature of the villainous billionaire, the scientific reality is less dramatic and more nuanced. While some widely publicized studies have suggested that wealth correlates with reduced empathy, more recent and empirically sound research has not only failed to replicate those findings, it has tended to find the opposite. Wealthy participants often display higher levels of strategic cooperation and generosity toward low-income individuals than the general population does.[1]

I can attest to this as someone who has succeeded at business and met a lot of other successful people. More often than not, the people who get ahead—whether by getting promoted to CEO or growing a company from scratch—are able to win people to their side, avoid making enemies, and have strong social skills. While the ogreish, Mr. Burns-type business mogul exists, he is the exception rather than the rule. Sociopathy is not a prerequisite to financial success, and if anything it's more of a liability than an asset, as it usually leads to colleagues, customers, or the law tearing you down long before you reach the top.

Even if it were true that billionaires are evil, demagoguing against them in this way is incredibly counterproductive, which makes the argument ineffective in addition to being wrong. Without exception, every single person on the receiving end of these attacks has internal rationalizations for their behavior that are far more convincing to them than any word ever uttered by the "billionaires shouldn't exist" crowd. As I said in the last chapter, the only defensible justification for the Bernies and Warrens of the world speaking about wealthy people the way they do is a belief that they can steamroll them. I contend this is difficult if not impossible, and so they'd catch more flies with honey than vinegar.

You may believe with every fiber of your being that billionaires are the devil incarnate, but you have to ask yourself what expressing that is getting you. Do diplomats start a negotiation by insulting one another? Do you air your decades of grievances against your mother

1. https://journals.plos.org/plosone/article?id=10.1371/journal.pone.0133193

when you're asking her to watch your kids? No? Then let's be strategic here as well.

It is far more effective to start from the position that billionaires are decent people with whom we have a reasonable disagreement. We should try to understand what drives their behavior and come up with good arguments for why they should change it. We should speak to them in a language of civility and common cause. We should try to persuade them that while their current course may seem optimal, it's actually not, and there's a better way for them to be.

Which brings us back to our original questions: why aren't the ultra wealthy more generous, and why don't we expect them to be? I think a lot of it boils down to the assumptions we make about their ethics and character. If we think of them as an evil force that must simply be overcome, then persuasion is futile and trying to force through higher taxes makes sense—maybe it's a long shot, but what other choice do we have? The inevitable response from the wealthy also makes sense, which is to perceive an enemy trying to forcibly take their property, and to use their considerable resources to fight back. Indeed, this is exactly what we see playing out today.

But if we think of the ultra wealthy as being basically like us, it's a totally different story. If they're like us, then we expect them to display a human level of kindness and generosity. Because we have that expectation, it makes sense to invest our efforts in persuasion first rather than going straight to force. The debate is no longer framed as "you're evil and I'm here to take your ill-gotten gains." Instead, we're making a nuanced and even-handed case for why greater generosity is better for everyone, including the wealthy. Whether they will be convinced remains to be seen, but it's reasonable to assume they'll at least let their guard down enough to listen, and that's a start.

I see three categories of persuasion that apply to wealth inequality: altruism, fear, and redirection. Without further ado, I'll get into each of them now.

8

PERSUASION BY ALTRUISM (AND PURE LOGIC)

"No one has ever become poor by giving."
— Anne Frank

Altruism is the unselfish concern for the well-being of others, and persuasion by altruism can be summed up in a sentence: "Wealthy people should be generous because it's the right thing to do." A natural way to make the case for altruism would be to paint a picture of how much better the world would be if the wealthy were more generous. However, since I've already devoted an entire chapter to that, I'm going to cover some new ground here. I'll start by comparing two potential paths for the ultra wealthy—Keeping vs. Giving—and then discuss some of the obstacles altruism faces, and how we might address them.

Keeping is what the vast majority of the ultra wealthy are currently doing. Sure, they might give away a bit at the margin, but they're keeping far more of their wealth than they need or will ever spend.

Giving is the altruistic path, and what I'm advocating. It means picking a Number that covers the most comfortable lifestyle one can imagine—and sure, that Number can have a healthy buffer added to it—and giving everything else away.

Which path leads to a better life?

The material comforts of each are identical, so there's nothing to say on that front. It really boils down to what the excess wealth is being used for, so let's examine that.

In the case of Keeping, a person's excess wealth is being used to... make them more wealthy. I'm not trying to be flip, that's literally all it's doing when you consider that, by definition, it's the wealth generating returns that will never be spent. If we want to be a bit more precise, we could say it's pushing up a person's rank on the Forbes 400 and potentially buying power and influence.

The question of why people seek power is far outside the scope of this book, let alone this chapter, and so rather than going into a long digression on it, I'll offer a couple of thoughts relevant to the discussion at hand. Broadly speaking, people seek power for two reasons: to enrich themselves, and to control people and events. For someone who starts out with power instead of wealth—a politician, for example—parlaying power into wealth might make sense. For someone who's already rich, it's a bit circular to use wealth to buy power to buy more wealth. Billionaires who give money to politicians in exchange for enacting policies that make them richer fall into this camp. They're chasing wealth for wealth's sake, to no particular end.

As for controlling people and events, this is a thornier issue. Let's put to the side those who seek power for nefarious purposes, which I hope we can agree is a bad thing to do. If we assume some billionaires seek power for noble purposes, the question is whether this is a good idea and how to get the best exchange rate on converting wealth to power. A "lower end" billionaire—someone worth less than $10 billion, say—really doesn't have enough money to buy meaningful power outright, and so they'd gain more by enhancing their public image. Ostentatious generosity would be a good way to do that and likely result in greater power and influence than trying to buy political or economic power directly.

At a higher net worth it becomes possible to buy real power, but just because you can do something doesn't mean you should. There are exactly zero examples from history of people who used wealth to buy power, gave nothing back, and are remembered fondly. Zero. Once the wealth evaporates, as it inevitably does, these people are either forgotten or remembered as villains. Those who transformed wealth into power and left a positive legacy—Augustus Caesar, Lorenzo de' Medici, and Andrew Carnegie, for example—did so by funding art, public works, and other forms of philanthropy. They might have chosen the Keeping path for a time, but we remember them because they ultimately chose Giving.

So let's turn to that.

Here's what Bill Gates's giving has done: immunized over 1 billion children, prevented an estimated 17 million deaths, and nearly eradicated polio.[1] He is the largest private funder of global health, and has saved more lives than all but a handful of people in human history.[2] Do you think he stays up at night regretting that his Forbes rank isn't higher? I don't.

While we can't all have the same impact as Gates, the calculus around Giving vs. Keeping is much the same for him as anyone else. In every case, it's the decision between keeping money one has no use for and using it to help others. Coming back to our question of which path leads to a better life, let's compare Keeping vs. Giving across a few dimensions to see which comes out on top. "Better life" is quite subjective, but the following categories seem like a reasonable basis for comparison.

Hedonic reward: This is a fancy way of saying "which is more fun at the time?" Again keeping in mind that the frills of wealth are the same on both paths (same private jet, same yacht), the hedonic

---

1. https://www.unicef.org/lac/en/press-releases/global-immunization-efforts-saved-154-million-lives-over-past-50-years

2. Determining who has saved the most lives in history is pretty fraught. Gates is behind the likes of Alexander Fleming—who discovered penicillin, which has saved hundreds of millions of lives—but he certainly ranks very high.

reward of Giving seems to be higher.[3] The Keeping path mostly entails continuing with the same things that led to a person having a high net worth in the first place—same meetings, same investor calls, and so on. At some point, doing the same old thing gets pretty boring, especially if the financial reward no longer has any impact on material comfort. Giving involves tackling new challenges, meeting new people, and having rewarding experiences—all with the ancillary benefit of saving lives and doing good in the world.

Winner: Giving.

Impact: Bill Gates has given away over $60 billion since 2000, and his current net worth is around $100 billion. Had he kept all that money, it's fair to say that with share price gains his net worth would be much higher—for the sake of argument, let's say he would be worth $400 billion. So who has more influence, cultural clout, and impact in the world: a $400 billion Gates with zero philanthropy, or a $100 billion Gates who's done all of the things listed above? I think it's the latter. The question really hinges on what he'd actually *do* with that extra $300 billion. The most reasonable guess is that it would just be sitting in his bank account, meaning it would have no purpose other than giving him the ability to brag that he has it. By comparison, generosity has put Gates in a class by himself when it comes to positive impact on the world. As such, he can open all the same doors as any other billionaire, plus a lot of others that would be closed to the rest.

Winner: Giving.

Legacy: Whatever else Gates does in his life, he will be remembered fondly for generations—maybe until the end of humanity—for the millions of lives he's saved and the immeasurable good he has done for mankind. As for the billionaires who give away nothing, who will remember them? Not even their own families at some point.

---

3. There is also a growing body of scientific evidence that "prosocial spending" (i.e. giving) makes people happy, and actually creates greater feelings of happiness and well-being than spending on oneself.

https://www.evidencebasedmentoring.org/the-benefits-to-the-brain-of-charitable-giving-prosocial-spending-and-happiness

Yes, we still talk about the fortunes of Rockefeller, Carnegie, and Vanderbilt, but the only reason we talk about them at all is because of the universities, libraries, and music halls that bear their names. It is their *generosity* that cemented their legacies, not the size of their fortunes.

Winner: Giving (and it's not even close).

This is why I call this persuasion by altruism *and* pure logic. By any conceivable measure, the generous billionaire wins. He's happier in the moment, carries more weight in the world, and has the far greater legacy.

And what do those who gave nothing have other than a higher rank in a magazine?

Nothing.

Altruism doesn't have to be a drag

One of the beliefs I held before I wrote this book—one that I imagine many people hold—was that altruism and selfishness lie at two opposite ends of a spectrum, just as losing and gaining do: being altruistic involves sacrifice, and being selfish generally entails the opposite. But as I thought more deeply about this, I realized that just as Newtonian physics works well for the day-to-day but fails at cosmic scales, this sort of zero-sum thinking works for most people but breaks down for the ultra wealthy.

An average earner might ask himself whether he'd be happier spending his $2,000 year-end bonus on a family vacation or donating it to charity. If he's being honest, he'd probably rather have the vacation, which is perfectly defensible. He might get some psychic benefit from the donation, but it would pale in comparison to the value he'd get from a vacation, such as fun, relaxation, and forming memories with his children.

For someone whose wealth exceeds her Number, this logic doesn't apply. By definition, she has more than enough to pay for all the vacations (and everything else) she could possibly want. She therefore wouldn't sacrifice anything by donating a windfall, and she wouldn't gain any material well-being by keeping it for herself.

Our instincts will always yell at us to hold onto as much as we can, but the truth is that once we've maxed out on the benefits of spending money on ourselves, it makes no logical sense to keep doing it. Even if all we care about is maximizing our own happiness and hedonic reward, we would still get better ROI elsewhere. This is unintuitive because most of us learn from an early age that spending money on ourselves brings pleasure. There's no obvious way to tell when we've hit the point where this stops being true, and so most of us continue doing what we've always done, oblivious to the fact that the payoff is gone. As I've stated before, this is why it's so important to know your Number—it tells you exactly where that stopping point is.

Once we've recognized that further spending on ourselves won't increase happiness, the next question is where to spend that money instead, and here we meet a second hurdle. The causes most associated with altruism—hunger, disease, human rights—are worthy but emotionally heavy. Most people avoid things that depress them, and if they believe that altruism requires them to invest their time and mental energy in such areas, they're likely to opt out.[4]

Instead of giving up, these people should get creative and find ways to be altruistic that are also positive and uplifting. What are they passionate about? If it's art, music, or sports, they could pay for local kids to learn those things. If it's entrepreneurship, they could provide grants to help people start businesses. If they love their city, they could pay to clean up graffiti, fill potholes, and upgrade playgrounds.

They could even target the problem of unhappiness itself. Loneliness is one of the greatest afflictions facing Americans today, and has become so widespread that the Surgeon General declared an "epidemic of loneliness and isolation" in 2023.[5] The ultra wealthy could

4. https://www.ovid.com/journals/jepge/abstract/10.1037/xge0001073~caring-is-costly-people-avoid-the-cognitive-work-of

5. https://www.hhs.gov/sites/default/files/surgeon-general-social-connection-advisory.pdf

step up here in ways that would address the problem while also improving their image and de-escalating class tensions.

In no particular order, here are a few ideas:

For an absolute pittance, Jeff Bezos could pay for an annual Festival Day in dozens of cities: free food, drinks, bands, etc. In addition to getting people out and meeting each other, he'd almost certainly recoup some of the cost in the form of goodwill toward Amazon.

Sergey Brin could rejuvenate America's "third places," many of which have shut down or fallen into disrepair in recent decades. Social clubs, fraternal organizations, recreation leagues, parks, and libraries all have a role to play in reducing isolation and loneliness.

Mark Zuckerberg could provide relief to single people looking for a match and parents in need of a break by subsidizing gym memberships, dating events, babysitters, and nights on the town.

Cities could invite their wealthy residents to donate to a "Let Kids be Kids" fund, which would pay for things like birthday parties, first bikes, summer camps, sports leagues, and so on. Speaking for myself, I'd love to get a monthly email with pictures and a recap of all the ways my donations helped underprivileged children enjoy the same things mine do.

The vast majority of the time we hear about the world's wealthiest people, it's in the context of running their business empires—jostling, fighting, and suing each other to become just a little bit richer and more powerful. This raises two questions. First, is any of this making them happier? And second, how differently might we feel about them if we occasionally saw them doing the kinds of things I've described here?

For all their striving to reach the very top of the wealth ladder, this group doesn't appear to be especially happy—they certainly don't seem any happier than the average person I know. I don't think it's crazy to imagine that at least some of them could meaningfully improve their lives by devoting a chunk of their wealth and time to improving the lives of others. And even if it didn't make them happier, even if putting a toy under every kid's Christmas tree brought them no joy at all, it would still do wonders for their public image and ease the growing hatred that regular people, particularly Gen Z, feel toward the ultra wealthy.

Put simply, altruism doesn't have to be a drag, and it can benefit the person doing the altruism. If a billionaire wants to bring joy to his community by sponsoring a series of block parties, and if doing so results in some people concluding that maybe he's not such a bad guy after all, I think that's a win on both counts.

Strategic altruism

The idea that altruism is a drag—something that comes at the expense of pleasure instead of being an accelerant of it—is one misconception worth dispelling. Another is that altruism is tainted or counts less if it's influenced by base considerations like self-interest, public perception, and selling.[6] The truth is that altruism can actually be more effective when layered with the sort of strategic thinking we more often associate with self-interest than altruism.

Bill Gates deserves all the praise in the world for his generosity, but if I could go back in time and offer him some advice, it would be this: start at home. I'm guessing few of you knew before reading this chapter that Gates has saved 17 million lives; I certainly didn't know it before I started my research. Because his generosity has been so focused on the third world, very few Americans are aware of it. They can't see what he's done, they don't know anyone he's helped, and they rarely hear about it—it might as well not exist. As a result, despite all of Gates's extraordinary work, he hasn't burnished the public image of the ultra wealthy or inspired many others to follow his example.

But imagine if he'd focused his efforts on the United States first, and chosen a highly visible issue that people really care about; housing affordability would be a good choice. In this alternate universe, hundreds of thousands of Americans would own a home

---

6. https://journals.sagepub.com/doi/abs/10.1177/0956797613504785

because of Gates, and millions more would personally know someone he helped. Instead of our current reality where some—but by no means most—of us are vaguely aware of Gates's philanthropy, there would be mass cultural awareness of the good that can be done by a generous billionaire.

How would this change the generosity landscape?

For one thing, other billionaires would take notice. They'd see Gates enjoying exactly the same benefits of wealth that he'd have anyway while also becoming a national hero and covering himself in glory. Many would want in on the action and follow his example. Instead of our current reality where only a handful of people have given away tens of billions of dollars, there might be dozens.

Someone thinking in terms of "pure altruism" would probably make the choice that Gates actually made. The situation of Africa's poor is far more dire than that of America's, and so if the question is where *Gates's* philanthropic dollars could save the most lives, the answer is Africa. But if we think strategically about how to do the most good overall, there's a strong argument that he should have spent those dollars in America. Not only would he inspire others to give more, it's likely Gates would respond to the greater level of praise and recognition by giving more himself. This strategy would save fewer lives in the short term but likely more in the long term. With a vastly larger pool of charitable giving, even if a smaller percentage went to third world vaccinations, total dollars given would be higher.[7]

It's too late to go back in time and run this counterfactual, but it's not too late to try it now. Some generous billionaire needs to pick a cause like housing or childcare and declare loudly and proudly, "I'm going to solve this problem for the American people." They need to

7. Readers familiar with Effective Altruism will hear some echoes in this section. While EA also argues that how we give matters enormously, it would reach the opposite conclusion here and choose Africa since philanthropic dollars go furthest in the developing world. We also diverge on how much people should give. EA advocates giving to the point of meaningful sacrifice, which is counterproductive since few people are willing to do that. My position is that capping wealth at one's Number is sufficient to address inequality, while also being much more palatable and likely to win converts. On both points, the EA position is admirable but, ironically, less effective.

make a point of puncturing the most damaging cultural idea we have about charity—that it should be done anonymously—and do the exact opposite. They must put their generosity on display, not for reasons of vanity, but to show others that philanthropy can be aspirational and sexy. By giving strategically, they could pull culture forward and inspire a movement.

9

PERSUASION BY FEAR

"How do I maintain control of my security force after my money is worthless?"

— Anonymous billionaire[1]

It is a historical fact that wealth inequality contributes to societal instability. Inequality was a factor in the fall of the Roman Republic, the French Revolution, the Russian Revolution, the Chinese Communist Revolution, and the Arab Spring. This should not come as a surprise. When a tiny minority has everything while a much larger group struggles, it's only natural that the majority will eventually resolve this situation by attacking the minority.

Given that the pattern of rising inequality leading to social unrest and violent revolution is as old as human civilization, one would expect to hear politicians, policy experts, and the ultra wealthy themselves warning of the threat. The volume and urgency of that

1. As related in *Survival of the Richest* by Douglas Rushkoff.

message should rise in tandem with inequality itself, which has now reached a level in the United States similar to that of France on the eve of Louis XVI's date with the guillotine.

But it's really crickets out there, isn't it?

A handful of billionaires such as Nick Hanauer, Ray Dalio, and Reid Hoffman are raising the alarm, but a far greater number have either said nothing or outright mocked the idea. To the extent that any of them are taking it seriously, the standard response is to build a bunker in a remote place like Hawaii or New Zealand.

There's a sick irony here. If we assume one of the main reasons to build an island compound is fear of societal collapse, it means the ultra wealthy *are* worried about this happening. They've just decided to act on that worry by... building a bunker in New Zealand.

I wonder how many of them have thought this through.

If things have gotten so bad that fleeing to New Zealand makes sense, it's unclear how many problems a bunker is actually going to solve. Does currency still work? If not, how do you pay your pilot to take you there? If it does, will he just accept it or will he make some additional demands, and will you be able to meet them? Will you be able to get to your plane in California, or off of it in Auckland, without being attacked by an angry mob? And assuming you can reach your bunker, what kind of life awaits you? Will your security team stay loyal? Kidnap you for ransom? Shoot you? Will you live out the rest of your days subsisting on canned food, ever on the lookout for bands of marauders trying to kill you and take your stuff?

Would you find yourself wishing you'd done more to prevent this?

Billionaire bunker mentality really stems from a collective action problem. One might say, "In a perfect world, we'd all band together and try to make things better in order to avoid a doomsday scenario. But that's unrealistic, and if I'm the only one who acts it solves nothing, so the next best thing is to build a bunker and look after myself." There's a certain logic to this, sure, but see above: when the shit hits the fan, what are the odds that you'll even get to your bunker safely, let alone manage a halfway decent existence once you get there?

If it were me, I'd put my efforts into working with my fellow billionaires to preserve what we have. After all, billionaires are the undisputed winners of *this society*, the one we live in right now. The last thing they should want is any sort of revolution that will replace it with something else. Instead of planning for some meager and terrifying post-apocalyptic existence, doesn't it make more sense to go all in on safeguarding society as it exists today?

I think there are a few reasons this doesn't happen. One is the collective action problem I just explained. Another is biology working against us. As discussed in Chapter 1, we're genetically programmed to have a hoarding mindset, with no counterbalancing instinct that says "I have enough." A generosity mindset would lead people to use their money to address inequality and prevent societal collapse; a hoarding mindset builds bunkers. Too many billionaires are still running hoarding software despite the fact that at their wealth, generosity is actually the optimal strategy.

People also underestimate this threat due to a host of cognitive biases. Optimism bias: the tendency to believe that negative events are less likely to happen to you personally than to others. Normalcy bias: the tendency to underestimate the likelihood and severity of disasters or crises because they haven't happened before in your experience. Availability heuristic: the tendency to judge the probability of events based on how easily examples come to mind (rare events like "the apocalypse" don't come to mind easily, so people underestimate their probability). Black swan bias: the tendency to be blind to rare, high-impact events because they're outside normal experience and statistical models.

In other words, people think the world can't end because it's never happened before. But really, they should realize it hasn't happened before *to them*. It's happened to plenty of other people—just ask the Romans. Revolutions ignite. Empires fall. It's not a common occurrence, but when it happens it tends to go very badly for most people, including the rich. And that speaks to another cognitive bias: wealthy people are used to being insulated from the worst that existence has to offer by their wealth, but societal collapse is one of those rare things where money may not be able to protect them. This is all the more reason to take the threat seriously, and act now while their money still can make a difference.

So how do we effect this change in mindset?

My vote is for pure, unadulterated rationality. The average billionaire has a net worth of $5.3 billion, and the odds of various outcomes we'd like to avoid happening in the next ten years are... whatever number seems reasonable to you.[2] For the sake of argument, I'll put the probability of a radical, anti-billionaire presidency at 20% and mass civil unrest at 5%.

If the ultra wealthy got on board with calculating their Number and giving away most or all of their excess wealth, they could drive down these probabilities. The attitude of the median American toward them would soften, as would the chances of them electing a demagogue of the hard left. Improvements to their material well-being would give them something to protect, and make them less likely to want to blow up the system.

So should billionaires hold onto all of that $5.3 billion, or give a lot of it away? What's the optimal strategy? What's the logical, self-interested thing to do?

They should give some of that money away. The excess wealth they're hanging onto is, by definition, unneeded and never going to be spent. That means it effectively has no value. Societal stability, on the other hand, is one of the most valuable things there is. Giving up something of no value for something of great value is an excellent trade. Even if it only pushes the odds of these negative outcomes down a little bit, it's still the obvious choice—but I suspect it pushes the odds down a lot.

"But this wealth does have value," some might say. "It's my legacy, my children's inheritance."

All I can say is: reconsider. If you want your legacy to be a litter of spoiled heirs who fritter away their lives spending your money, have at it. There are more than enough cautionary tales from history of

---

2. https://www.forbes.com/sites/chasewithorn/2025/04/01/forbes-39th-annual-worlds-billionaires-list-more-than-3000-worth-16-trillion/

such lives ending in addiction and ignominy that you should have known better. If you love your children, it's far kinder to follow Warren Buffett's advice and give them "enough so they can do anything, but not enough that they can do nothing." This gives them a chance to be their own person, and not just an heir. And though it may seem counterintuitive, being generous with your fortune secures your children's future better than leaving all of it to them. After all, one of the greatest threats they face is a populist revolution in which they'll have to pay the debt incurred by your excess. Generosity reduces this risk.

Billionaires must ask themselves what they need to live like a billionaire. Many will answer with a single word: money. But they actually need two things: money *and* societal stability. The ultra wealthy would do well to start thinking of societal stability as a resource that's just as important as money and requires effort to maintain. You can't enjoy your billions if the world is on fire.

The good news is that while societal stability isn't free, it is cheap. How can I be so sure? Again, it all comes back to the Number concept. Billionaires weren't going to spend this money anyway, so it effectively has no value *to them*. But it has enormous value for the people receiving it. They will see this generosity and come to realize that billionaires are not some evil monster to be destroyed. And this, coupled with real gains in their quality of life, will take the temperature down. The ultra wealthy can go on living *exactly as they do now* while significantly reducing the risk of the worst possible outcomes.

It's an absolute no-brainer.

10

PERSUASION BY REDIRECTION

"After a certain point, money is just a way of keeping score."
— Sam Zell

If we want wealthy people to pour themselves into generosity with the same enthusiasm as making money, we need to understand exactly why the latter is so intoxicating to them (and the former isn't). Many assume it's the accumulation of wealth itself that drives them, which not only doesn't translate to generosity but is antithetical to it. I think this assumption is wrong. While wealth accumulation is usually the primary motivator in the early stages of a wealthy person's career, it recedes over time and ultimately becomes incidental, a byproduct of one's true drives.

So what *does* motivate them? Why do they keep accumulating wealth if it's not just the money?

"Default programming" is the most succinct way to explain a lot of it. They're doing what biology, history, and the example of their peers are all telling them to do. But there are other important motivators as well, such as competition, recognition, and the feeling of accomplishment—keeping score, in other words.

If we can better understand how making money serves as an outlet for these psychological drives, we can devise ways for generosity to do it as well. With the proper incentive structures in place, wealthy people will naturally redirect their mental energy away from accumulation and toward generosity—no shaming, nagging, or finger-wagging required. They'll just do it themselves.

Competition and recognition

Despite being fairly tongue-in-cheek, the quote at the start of this chapter speaks volumes about the mindset of the world's wealthiest people, which is often misunderstood by the media and general public. In both the news and everyday conversation, the way we talk about how the ultra wealthy accumulate money is very similar to how we talk about our own wealth. We wonder what they'll buy with it, or what they'll be able to afford if they have more of it. But as we've discussed a couple times now, you can afford pretty much everything with a billion dollars, and certainly with two. Billionaires know this, which means they're not continuing to amass wealth so they can afford more stuff.

They're doing it to win.

If life is a game where the objective is to maximize one's score, many wealthy people see making money as being worth more points than anything else, and so they naturally try very hard at it. It's also critical to understand that the most successful people in the world—in business, sports, and any other field of human endeavor—tend to be extremely competitive. It's a major part of how they got to be successful in the first place, and it never goes away no matter how rich they get.

Today, many billionaires compete to be the richest, and few—other than Warren Buffett and Bill Gates, perhaps—compete to be the most generous. We must therefore ask ourselves why accumulation lends itself to competitiveness, and generosity doesn't. What is generosity lacking?

Measurement, for one thing. It's impossible to compete over something if you can't measure it, and impossible to be recognized as being the best if you can't compete.

When asked why he wanted to climb Mount Everest, the English mountaineer George Mallory famously replied, "Because it's there." In the same spirit, the world's wealthiest people have competed for the last 40 years to stand atop the Forbes 400 because it's there. Being able to buy anything in the world is nice, but eventually even that loses its novelty; working one's way up the Forbes list presents an evergreen challenge, something to strive for. Not only does this leaderboard help billionaires keep score, it actually makes them richer. Its existence motivates them to grow their wealth even more in order to increase their rank.

Knowing this, it's striking that we have not engineered a way for the ultra wealthy to express their competitiveness via philanthropy. To start a similar virtuous cycle where billionaires compete to be the most generous, we need a **Giving Index** for them to stand atop. This creates a new game to play, a new way for billionaires to compete and make their mark on the world. With sufficient adoption, billionaires would no longer see generosity as costing them rank on the Forbes list but increasing their rank on a list that carries more goodwill and cultural clout.

There is currently no centralized source of truth for charitable giving. Various organizations track small pieces of it, but there is nothing like the Forbes 400 or Bloomberg Billionaires Index in terms of comprehensiveness or mass cultural penetration. We should change that by creating a Giving Index, a universal source of truth for charitable giving. In its first iteration, it would simply track the giving of the world's wealthiest people. Over time, it could be integrated with all of the world's charities, creating a comprehensive database of who needs money, who's giving it, and the problems they're solving.

The value of this is twofold. First, as already mentioned, it will spur friendly competition among the wealthy to be more generous.

Second, as every businessperson knows, that which gets measured gets improved. Better data virtually always leads to better results, and the world of philanthropy is in desperate need of better data and a more results-oriented approach. Many people feel that their donations are wasted, or that the problems we're trying to solve will remain intractable no matter how much we spend. Unlike in business, where we can generally see the fruits of our investment in very real terms, charitable giving often feels more like stemming the tide than solving problems. We give because we feel like we should, but for the above reasons many of us get little satisfaction from it, which predictably results in less giving.

And that brings me to my next point.

The feeling of accomplishment

Everyone knows the feeling of accomplishment that comes from solving problems, but there is a unique and addictive flavor of it that one experiences when running a business. Sometimes you face a problem that is existential—solve it or go out of business. Other times, solving a problem takes you and your organization to another level, opening opportunities you never imagined before.

Sometimes it's both.

In 1999, Google faced a problem. Demand for its search engine was growing so fast that meeting it with off-the-shelf servers would bankrupt them. So they innovated. They built their own servers with the cheapest parts they could find, including corkboard and velcro, and developed innovative new software to squeeze every last drop of utility from them. And it worked. Not only did they solve their server problem for a fraction of what it otherwise would have cost, their insight that you could serve web traffic using thousands of cheap, unreliable machines instead of robust mainframe computers paved the way for modern cloud computing.

As Larry Page personally tended to the server racks repairing ribbon cables with twist ties, he might have had a vague idea of his impending billionairedom. But I'd place a very large bet that he wasn't fantasizing about money. He was calculating how many milliseconds the latest code push would shave off Google's response time.

This obsessive mindset is what makes great entrepreneurs great. And the object of this obsession is almost always their own companies. Why? Not because they're greedy, not because the only thing they care about is money. It's because the only problems a person can solve are the ones they're aware of, and they're aware of the problems at their company. It's because people want to tackle problems that can definitively be solved, optimize things that can be optimized, and business problems tend to be this way. In the beginning, yes, the financial rewards matter. But the reason these great minds keep toiling away year after year is not because they're slavering over their 48 billionth dollar—it's because they want to fix, optimize, improve, figure stuff out, get wins, and show everyone how smart they are. They want to get shit done, and this is where they can do it.

There's an unmet demand here, and it presents a massive opportunity for the generosity movement. Entrepreneurs continue to chase meaning at their companies long past the point of diminishing returns and expired novelty. They need a new game to play.

Let's keep using Larry Page as an example. He's an engineer at heart, and I imagine he was happiest in Google's early days when he got to personally solve engineering problems. As the company became enormous, it got harder for him to contribute that way. These days he adds value by directing resources and making decisions about engineering problems that others will solve. This isn't as rewarding as what he was doing before, but it's all he's got. Many entrepreneurs find themselves in this situation—no longer writing code or closing deals themselves, relegated to approving budgets at board meetings. Watching their companies continue to grow delivers some satisfaction, and their increasing net worth provides tepid reassurance that they're not completely wasting their time, but it's nothing like the visceral thrills of old.

Now let's imagine that through the Giving Index, we have an

enormous list of humanitarian and social problems waiting to be solved, including the exact cost to solve them. For example:

- Eradicate malaria in... Nigeria: $X; Tanzania: $Y; Uganda: $Z, etc.
- End hunger in... [list of countries]
- Make home ownership affordable for X% of households in... [list of states]
- Address the shortage of plumbers in... [list of cities]

If we multiply the various types of problems—food, health, housing, education, childcare, etc.—by the thousands of places they need to be solved, we're talking about a list that could run into the millions. Now we have something that problem-solvers can really sink their teeth into.

Someone like Larry Page could apply the same "Google server mindset" to curing disease. Maybe he starts with addressing malaria in a small country. During the initial pilot, he figures out how to procure mosquito nets cheaper and deploy them more efficiently; now he's able to tackle the next country for less money. As his success builds, maybe he decides to fund research to stop mosquitoes from spreading malaria at a genetic level. Larry famously likes to set crazy, ambitious goals, so he should have at it—completely eradicate one of the world's deadliest diseases.

Or imagine a billionaire hedge fund manager who has decided to embrace generosity and live by his Number. He made his fortune by exploiting market inefficiencies that others missed, going against conventional wisdom, seeing things differently. Now, instead of endlessly growing a pile of money he'll never spend, he uses his unique skillset to start a Generosity Hedge Fund. His goal? Figure out how to maximize the societal return from every dollar donated using the same keen intellect and creativity that built his fortune. If this sounds fanciful, keep in mind that most billionaire hedge fund managers are many years removed from incremental wealth impacting their living standards, and are well into the phase of wealth as a means of keeping score. In today's culture, they might express this with something ostentatious like a vintage car collection, but such displays are pointless in a world that has moved on from admiring someone simply for being rich. As cultural values change, so too does the object of the hedge fund manager's game, from maximizing net worth to maximizing societal impact.

And this game isn't just for billionaires. With a searchable index, the millionaire doctor who lives down the street might realize she has enough to endow an electrician apprenticeship program in her city. Instead of just complaining about how hard it is to find good help these days, she's doing something about it and helping her fellow citizens find lucrative careers in the process. She's solving a problem.

Tying it all together

Dream with me for a minute.

It's a few years from now, and the Giving Index is integrated into most of the world's charities. We know who's giving, how much, and where their money is going. We can also see in detail exactly what each charity is trying to do and how well they're doing it.

Instead of vague mission statements like "making housing more affordable for the working class" or "fighting tuberculosis in impoverished countries," charities list specific, solvable problems. Instead of setting fundraising targets based on what they think is feasible, they show a price tag. If the price is high, they list it unapologetically while never forgetting to add that they'd be thrilled if some clever person can figure out how to do it for less.

And the ultra wealthy step up. Gone is the antiquated notion that giving should be done anonymously, which, whatever its virtues, provided cover for those who gave little or nothing. They have realized that to maximize generosity, they must embrace a new social norm: broadcasting their giving in order to set a positive example and create social pressure for others to be generous as well.

In this world, billionaires compete over giving factor and total dollars given, and rack up achievements like they're playing a video game.[1] They tick through problems they discover in the Giving Index: childcare in this state, community college in that state, relief from natural disasters as they come up. They apply a business mindset and find ways to solve problems faster, cheaper, better. Philanthropic breakthroughs get media attention, inspiring others to pile in. People who are now able to afford a house, start a family, send their kid to college, or pay for a life-changing operation post videos to say thank you.

It gives you the warm-and-fuzzies, doesn't it?

This *can* happen. The first step is setting up the playing field and scoring system: comprehensive tracking of charitable giving, clear problem statements, and the ability to resolve those problems as solved. Next, we need to demonstrate to wealthy people that they can get at least as much juice from this game as they've historically done by chasing a higher net worth. That's it. With these pieces in place, we can rely on the ultra wealthy's competitiveness, desire for recognition, and love of problem-solving to take over.

We should never forget that the entrepreneurial mindset is a *good thing*. It's more responsible than anything else for building this country and making it the envy of the world. We can never suppress it and we'd be insane to try. Instead, we need to lean into it, harness it, and redirect it toward generosity.

---

1. Recall from Chapter 4 that giving factor is a way of expressing lifetime giving as a percentage of net worth. Someone who has given away $50 million and has a net worth of $100 million would have a 50% giving factor.

11

WHY PERSUASION WORKS BETTER THAN FORCE

"You catch more flies with honey than vinegar."
— Mom

Over the last three chapters, we've walked through a number of arguments one can make to persuade the ultra wealthy to be more generous. We can show them that it's the right thing to do (altruism), and we can also make the case that it's both the sensible (fear) and rewarding (redirection) choice. To round out the case for persuasion, I'd like to tick through some reasons it will be more effective than trying to force tax legislation through Congress.

People want to choose, they don't want to be forced

If we can persuade the wealthy to address inequality, we'll have a willing partner who will work with us to advance a common cause. If we try to force them, the most likely outcome is that we'll simply lose to their superior lobbying; the second most likely is that we'll succeed in the short term while creating an insurgent enemy who won't rest until our victory is overturned. It's tempting to use force when we believe our cause is righteous, but we need to be careful not to delude ourselves that doing so will be easy or effective. As difficult as persuasion may seem, we should try our hardest to make it work before abandoning it in favor of force.

Imagine your neighbors are having a loud party and keeping you awake. What's the best way to handle it? Option A is to call the cops. Option B is to knock on their door or text them first, ask them to be quiet, and only call the cops if that doesn't work. Most people will choose Option B. Even if going straight to the cops works—and there's no guarantee that it will—you've nuked your relationship with your neighbor forever. It's much better to try to reason with someone first, then escalate if that fails.

Let people choose to do the right thing before trying to force them.

It neuters anti-tax and anti-government arguments

The problem with forced redistribution through taxes is not the redistribution, it's who's doing it. Governments have amply earned their reputation for fiscal incompetence, and the wealthy are right to point out that raising taxes without looking at the other side of the ledger only exacerbates the problem. Those of us who have run a business are particularly allergic to the government's approach toward money. Every day, we have to think carefully about how we spend our resources, ever conscious that a single misstep could bankrupt our company—this discipline drives efficiency and better results. There's none of that in government. When there's a cost overrun, politicians just raise taxes, print more money, or sink the nation further into debt.

I have some questions for politicians who want to raise taxes. What is the appropriate size of government? What's a reasonable amount to spend on the military, healthcare, and entitlements? How do we ensure that the government spends money responsibly? In fairness to them, there is no answer they could give that would be broadly accepted. The problem is that so few of them even try, which undercuts their arguments for raising taxes.

I'm sympathetic to people who worry about enabling government waste; I'm unsympathetic to those who refuse to give directly to people who need it. When we remove the cover provided by anti-government arguments, we can see who the real free marketers are, and who is just being greedy.

20% vs. 100%

This one's dead simple. As explained in Chapter 6, only about 20% of federal tax revenues go toward programs that address inequality; the other 80% pays for the military, interest payments, and effectively insolvent entitlement programs with little accountability to the taxpayer. When wealthy people give directly, almost all of it, minus a small percentage for overhead, goes toward solving the problem. If you're looking for the best bang for your buck, voluntary generosity wins.

Unleash the power of smart people with good ideas

Call me a hopeless capitalist, but I just think businesspeople will do a better job of addressing inequality than politicians. If you've ever read about Steve Jobs, you know that what drove him more than anything else was revolutionizing industries and doing things other people said were impossible. He put a thousand songs in our pockets with the iPod and then changed the world forever when he launched the iPhone, which traditionalists thought would fail because it lacked a physical keyboard.[1]

If we can channel this same mindset and passion toward philanthropy, we'll quickly find that we've set our sights far too low on

1. It seems crazy now that people thought this, but TechCrunch, Steve Ballmer (CEO of Microsoft), and many others did.

what's possible. Government may be able to tackle this problem on its own, but if we're looking for real breakthroughs we need innovators to engage. Taxes won't do that; persuasion by redirection will.

It's actually the better option for raising taxes as well

Most of this book has framed persuasion and taxes as being at odds —you either pursue one or the other. In reality, focusing on persuasion first makes it easier to enact better tax policies. Today's ultra wealthy see higher taxes as an attack they must defend against. By contrast, someone who has moved on from maximizing net worth will be far less resistant to higher taxes. At that point, the idea of paying down the national debt and providing their children a brighter future becomes more attractive than hanging onto money they have no use for.

This change in mindset would apply to all forms of taxation as well as corporate governance in general. The whole point of offshore corporate tax dodges is to inflate a company's share price, but if leadership has moved past a "maximize wealth at all costs" mindset, there's no reason to keep doing this. Similarly, today's CEO might do something morally questionable because it will push up the company's stock by five percent; if that same CEO picks a Number and is no longer solely focused on maximizing his wealth, he's more likely to listen to his conscience.

SIMPLY PUT, persuasion wins. It avoids the political backlash of forced redistribution, deploys resources more efficiently, and creates willing partners rather than bitter enemies. Most importantly, it's the only approach that can actually change our cultural ideas around wealth. Without it, we're locked in a forever war with the wealthy where the best we can hope for is marginal victories punctuated by constant setbacks. But if we lead with persuasion, we can start a cultural shift where the wealthy choose generosity on their own. This is the path to durable change—the only path.

I rest my case.

12

RETHINKING WEALTH AND GENEROSITY

"We each come by the gifts we have to offer by an infinite series of influences and lucky breaks we can never fully understand."
— MacKenzie Scott

Our instincts to hoard resources come from millions of years of evolution, and most of human existence has been a story of scarcity and struggle. Biology and history have shaped a society primed to accept inequality, one in which the rich endlessly accumulate wealth and everyone else accepts that as normal. But today, this status quo is starting to buckle under the weight of the information age. Since 1990, the number of billionaires has climbed from about 260 to over 3,000; the richest among them went from having single digits of billions to hundreds of billions. Not only did the internet create vast numbers of incomprehensible fortunes at unprecedented speed, it made it possible for the first time to directly observe the lives of the ultra wealthy. Our front-row seat to this explosion of net worth catapulted wealth inequality from something few people talked about to one of the most urgent and debated issues of our time.

Given the scale and speed of this change, it's unsurprising that we've struggled to make sense of it. This is why various groups can look at the same set of facts and arrive at wildly different conclusions. The people who dismiss inequality as an issue are correct when they say that societies have always been unequal. Those who want to legislate billionaires out of existence are also on firm ground in pointing out that we now have individuals whose wealth has grown to rival that of entire nations, and that this happened while real wages in the developed world have been stagnant for decades. As for the billionaires themselves, they can be forgiven for their bewilderment over the fact that they were generally admired as recently as the mid-2000s, while today they're increasingly seen as parasites.

All three groups have a point, but amid the whirlwind of change they've also gotten some things wrong. Yes, inequality has always existed, but it's now approaching a level that threatens to fundamentally break the economy. Yes, the explosion of wealth at the top is a problem we must address, but rejecting capitalism is not the answer. Yes, public opinion on billionaires has soured, but that shouldn't be surprising given how much the playing field has shifted in their favor.

Instead of pointing these things out and trying to build consensus around a shared understanding of the problem, our politicians, academics, and influencers have monomaniacally focused on tax policy. Never mind that a large population denies the issue and the unconvinced wealthy will use every ounce of their enormous power to fight back—let's just try to jam through higher taxes and hope for the best. This hasn't worked, and it's not going to work.

To move forward, we need to recalibrate to modern reality and coalesce on a message that's unifying, actionable, and inspiring. We need to acknowledge the forces that have brought us to this pass while having faith that we can push past them toward something better. Yes, biology drives us to hoard resources. It also drives us to forcibly procreate and kill rivals, and yet we've been able to check those instincts in order to live in a civilized society. Yes, the prevailing example of history is hoarding, but for 99% of it we didn't have Enlightenment ideals or post-industrial abundance; just because medieval kings were selfish doesn't mean modern billionaires have to be. Yes, some level of inequality is inevitable under capitalism, but that doesn't mean we should abandon the system or vilify the wealthy; it means we should closely monitor inequality and try to keep it within a healthy range.

Intelligent people can hold two opposing thoughts in their head at once: the ultra wealthy have been selfish, and they're also key to our prosperity. Almost everyone in a society has a comparable capacity to do labor, but only a tiny percentage are willing to work long hours for no pay and gamble their future on a new idea. Millions of people have a livelihood and billions receive things of value from companies like Microsoft, Google, and Amazon, and this is true regardless of their founders' track records on taxes and philanthropy. Some of you will insist that social media is tearing us apart, data centers are destroying the environment, and all of these companies' founders have far too much money. However valid these concerns may be, the fact is that no one forced us to use their products—we wanted them. We were happy to give these companies our money, or in the case of search, receive something of previously unimaginable utility for free.

It's fine to question how much money these moguls really need and to call out those who give little or nothing back, but it's absurd to accuse them of stealing from us and delusional to pretend that our current situation is some searing indictment of capitalism. The cold hard truth is that the only reason we have wealth to redistribute at all is because of capitalism, and billionaires are a natural byproduct of our prosperity. Communist societies don't have to worry about inequality, but that's only because everyone is poor.[1] However aggrieved you feel against the wealthy, rejecting capitalism is not the answer.

This is the critical point: we need to agree on a message that's pro-

1. Minus a handful of oligarchs close to the leader, of course.

capitalism and sympathetic to those at the top, while also stating in the clearest possible terms that our current level of inequality is unsustainable and must be addressed. If we can reach consensus on this, we can move on from the fractious arguments of today and wage an influence campaign to persuade the wealthy of the following: first, endless accumulation is a sociological relic that they should seek to overcome. Second, they are entitled to their lives of opulence but should give away their excess wealth for the common good and to safeguard future stability.

There are a few tactical things that all of us can do to push culture in this direction. Stop consuming Instagram wealth porn and feeding a social media environment that fetishizes money and materialism. Praise billionaires as loudly as possible when they model generosity. Never miss an opportunity to point out to your friends and family how unnecessary it is to have multiple billions of dollars, and how much better the world would be if more people agreed with you.

But by far the single most important call to action for the middle class is to amplify the message. You can't force wealthy people to be generous, but you can create a cultural climate where conversations about wealth and generosity become unavoidable for them. The first time they hear about the concept of limiting net worth to their Number, many will respond with a grunt or a dismissive "interesting thought." After the 50th time, it becomes impossible to avoid seriously engaging with the argument, and some percentage of those who do will be persuaded. The more wealthy people start living by their Number, the more their positive example will influence others to join them. A snowball will become an avalanche.

For this to happen we need to maximize both the reach and frequency of this message. Put simply: **if you like the ideas in this book, spread them.**

A message for billionaires

You have reached an unassailable position, or nearly so. Material comfort, novel experiences, health, longevity, knowledge—you have greater access to these things than anyone who has ever lived. The only thing that could go wrong is mass social upheaval. Is that possible? Yes. In fact, it's never failed to happen when conditions get to a certain point.

We've been heading toward this precipice for decades, and things are only accelerating. When AI automates someone's job, they lose their salary and economic viability, and it flows to billionaires. The person who lost these things needed them, and the person who got them didn't. Maybe that's just the free market at work, but at some point people are going to hit their limit and start trying to take things back. When that happens, you might find yourself wishing you could go back and do things differently. But it will be too late.

Even if you had to make real sacrifices to avoid this fate, it would be the most obvious decision in the world to make them. But no one's asking for that. Keep your private jet, your yacht, your beautiful homes. Live exactly as you do now. Consider whatever is left over—and if you're worth billions of dollars, that's a lot—as a down payment on a happier, safer, and more stable society.

Maximizing your net worth isn't serving you. It's driving you to sprint on the hedonic treadmill, chasing a feeling of "enough" that never comes. If you're self-made, ask yourself whether you're happier now or years ago when you were building your fortune and wealth was ahead of you instead of defining you. If you're an heir, tell us what it feels like to sit on unearned and unspendable wealth while those born to poorer parents struggle with problems you could easily solve.

Whatever pleasures your wealth brings, it will still bring them when scaled down to your Number. The portion you give away will bring more: fulfillment from helping others, satisfaction from solving problems, peace of mind from greater societal stability. You face a simple choice: continue amassing wealth that you know deep down isn't making you any happier, and pray that the growing rage won't touch you or your family—or start giving some of it away. I can't guarantee the latter will make you happier or more fulfilled, though I'd say it's a safe bet it will. I can guarantee it will help sustain an economic system you have a more vested interest in than anyone.

The paradox is that getting more doesn't always mean you're winning, and giving doesn't have to mean losing. The only thing you win by maximizing your net worth is a higher rank in a magazine. By giving, you can do real good in the world and leave a legacy that will make your descendants proud to bear your name. The drive to endlessly accumulate comes from primal instincts rooted in the savanna; the realization that you can override this programming comes from reason.

There was a time when iconic American companies like General Motors spoke with patriotic pride in their annual report about how much they paid in taxes.[2] While I'm ambivalent about solving inequality with taxes, I can't help but feel that we lost something when we abandoned these values. It *is* our civic duty to care about others and to contribute to a strong, durable society. We should be proud that we are in a position to leave this country better than we found it. Such sentiments are unfashionable in corporate America these days, but who says we can't bring them back? The world would be better off if we did.

And finally, try to be humble. I chose this chapter's opening quote to remind us that there's more to success than smarts and hard work —there's a great deal of luck too. You could have been born into third world poverty, or with a disability. The chance encounter that sparked your business might have never happened. The technological wave you rode might have crested a little earlier or a little later and passed you by. But for whatever reason, you were in the right place at the right time, and you were born with the requisite level of intelligence, perseverance, and work ethic. It might not have happened, but it did.

What better way to express your gratitude for your exceptional good fortune than to pay it forward?

---

2. https://babel.hathitrust.org/cgi/pt?id=osu.32435027473941&seq=29

A better future is coming

In his 1903 book *Light Waves and their Uses*, American physicist Albert Michelson observed, "The more important fundamental laws and facts of physical science have all been discovered, and these are now so firmly established that the possibility of their ever being supplanted in consequence of new discoveries is exceedingly remote." Few today have heard of this book, but almost everyone has heard of a discovery published by another physicist named Albert just two years later: the special theory of relativity.

The vast majority of us fall prey to a cognitive bias—sometimes called chronocentrism, presentism, or the end-of-history illusion—where we assume the current moment represents the pinnacle of our species, and the future will bring nothing more than minor improvements. The irony is that we can easily see the evolution in cultural mores that distinguish 2026 from 2006, 1986, and 1966, yet when it comes to 2046, most of us assume our values will basically be the same as now. It's hard to imagine not only that the world will be different someday, but people will look at things that seem perfectly normal to us as old-fashioned, backward, even barbaric.

Yet there can be no doubt this is coming.

Humanity has a proven track record of moving on from bad ideas in favor of better ones. In no particular order, here are some things we've mostly abandoned as a species: slavery, child labor, putting cocaine in children's medicine, divination, animal sacrifice, human sacrifice, bloodletting, doctors doing surgery without washing their hands, doctors endorsing cigarette brands, cigarette ads in general, smoking in general (in many countries), denying women the vote, denying girls education, racial segregation, foot binding, corsets, lobotomies, bloodsport, witch trials, torture, public executions, corporal punishment, dueling, criminalizing interracial marriage, the seven-day work week, dumping industrial waste into rivers, CFCs, lead paint, and those old-timey bicycles with the giant front wheel.

The lesson? Cultural change is not only possible but inevitable. That means that even if our traditional notions of wealth are creaking under the weight of modern reality—and they are—we have every reason to be optimistic that better ideas will come along. If we can all start singing from the same hymn book and having a more productive conversation on the topic of inequality, we can hasten that change.

One of the words I hear a lot when I share my ideas is "irrational." It's irrational to believe the wealthy can be persuaded toward generosity, irrational to advocate for a solution that doesn't involve force, irrational to think our cultural ideas on wealth and inequality can evolve.

I contend that it's actually our current attitudes toward wealth that are irrational—we only assume they're rational because they're so pervasive. When we examine them, we can see that they're an evolutionary and historical holdover, sociological scars from a scarce and meager past. They're out of step with our current age of abundance, and this creates a dissonance many of us feel but can't quite express. This is our intuition telling us we're ready to move on from them.

There's nothing rational about spending the limited time we have on this earth working to amass wealth we'll never spend, nothing rational about millions dying from preventable diseases while a lucky few sit on fortunes that can't be counted. It's the things we accept as normal today that are irrational, not the idea that we can be better. Future generations will see this clearly.

ACKNOWLEDGEMENTS

I would like to thank:

My parents (Louise and Joe) and the place I grew up (Santa Cruz, California) for teaching me strong middle class values.

My friends and family who read advance copies and provided feedback. Sorry for all the "wait, read this version instead."

My wife, Irina, and my two boys, Finn and Jack, for everything.

All the people who read this far.

If you enjoyed this book, please share it.

APPENDIX A: REFERENCED MATERIALS

Further Reading on the Problem of Wealth Inequality

"Economic Inequality Seen as Major Challenge Around the World." Pew Research Center. https://www.pewresearch.org/global/2025/01/09/economic-inequality-seen-as-major-challenge-around-the-world/

"Inequality — Bridging the Divide." United Nations. https://www.un.org/en/un75/inequality-bridging-divide

"Nine Charts about Wealth Inequality in America." Urban Institute. https://apps.urban.org/features/wealth-inequality-charts/

"Rising Inequality: A Major Issue of Our Time." Brookings Institution. https://www.brookings.edu/articles/rising-inequality-a-major-issue-of-our-time/

"The Rise of Income and Wealth Inequality in America: Evidence from Distributional Macroeconomic Accounts." American Economic Association. https://www.aeaweb.org/articles?id=10.1257/jep.34.4.3

"Trends in income and wealth inequality." Pew Research Center. https://www.pewresearch.org/social-trends/2020/01/09/trends-in-income-and-wealth-inequality/

"Wealth Inequality in the United States." Institute for Policy Studies. https://inequality.org/facts/wealth-inequality/

"What Is Wrong with Inequality?" Oxford Open Economics. https://academic.oup.com/ooec/article/3/Supplement_1/i4/7259874

Referenced Books

Carnegie, Dale. *How to Win Friends and Influence People*. 1936

Rushkoff, Douglas. *Survival of the Richest*. 2022.

Schroeder, Alice. *The Snowball: Warren Buffett and the Business of Life*. 2008

Stevenson, Gary. *The Trading Game: A Confession*. 2024.

Twist, Lynne. *The Soul of Money*. 2003.

Chapter Notes

Preface

"Majorities of Americans say wealth inequality is a problem and want government intervention." YouGov. https://yougov.com/en-us/articles/53821-majorities-americans-say-wealth-inequality-is-problem-want-government-intervention-january-2-5-2026-economist-yougov-poll

Chapter 2

"Earners vs. Owners." Prof G Media. https://www.profgalloway.com/earners-vs-owners/

"Gen Z's Definition of Financial Success." Fortune. https://fortune.com/2024/11/23/gen-z-financial-success-definition-salary-net-worth-millennials-gen-x-boomers/

"Good genes are nice, but joy is better." Harvard University. https://news.harvard.edu/gazette/story/2017/04/over-nearly-80-years-harvard-study-has-been-showing-how-to-live-a-healthy-and-happy-life/

"Good Social Relationships Are the Most Consistent Predictor of a Happy Life." Stanford University. https://ccare.stanford.edu/press_posts/good-social-relationships-are-the-most-consistent-predictor-of-a-happy-life/

"Here's the Happiness Research that Stands Up to Scrutiny." Scientific American. https://www.scientificamerican.com/article/heres-the-happiness-research-that-stands-up-to-scrutiny/

"The Amount and Source of Millionaires' Wealth (Moderately) Predicts Their Happiness." Harvard Business School. https://www.hbs.edu/ris/Publication%20Files/donnelly%20zheng%20haisley%20norton_26bec744-c924-4a28-8439-5a74abe9c8da.pdf

"The Role of Self-Determination in Well-Being." Psychology Today. https://www.psychologytoday.com/us/blog/click-here-for-happiness/202209/the-role-of-self-determination-in-well-being

Chapter 3

"Bay Area Sees Huge Influx of Billionaire Residents—Cementing Its Status as World's Wealth Capital." SFGate. https://www.sfgate.com/realestate/article/bay-area-sees-huge-influx-of-billionaire-20265888.php

"CPI Inflation Calculator." U.S. Bureau of Labor Statistics. https://www.bls.gov/data/inflation_calculator.htm

"Millionaires by City 2025." Henley Global. https://www.henleyglobal.com/publications/wealthiest-cities-2025/top-50-cities-millionaires

"Robin Williams' Marin Mansion Sells." San Francisco Chronicle. https://www.sfchronicle.com/realestate/article/robin-williams-mansion-sale-photos-20058958.php

Chapter 4

"Heterogeneity of the Carnegie Effect." The Journal of Human Resources. https://jhr.uwpress.org/content/54/3/726

"Majority of wealthy parents say big inheritances can harm children – Rathbones." The Intermediary. https://theintermediary.co.uk/2025/08/majority-of-wealthy-parents-say-big-inheritances-can-harm-children-rathbones/

"The psychology of wealth." Pictet. https://www.pictet.com/global/en/psychology-of-wealth

"When too much is not enough: Inherited wealth and the psychological meaning of money." Columbia University. https://business.columbia.edu/sites/default/files-efs/pubfiles/2669/Too%20much%20not%20enough.pdf

Chapter 5

"A Purpose-Driven Fund to End Extreme Poverty by 2030." Brookings Institution. https://www.brookings.edu/articles/a-purpose-driven-fund-to-end-extreme-poverty-by-2030/

"Air Quality." Office of Environmental Quality and Transboundary Issues. https://www.state.gov/key-topics-office-of-environmental-quality-and-transboundary-issues/air-quality/

"Ammonia Emission Controls as a Cost-Effective Strategy for Reducing Atmospheric Particulate Matter in the Eastern United States." Environmental Science & Technology, 2007. https://pubs.acs.org/doi/10.1021/es060379a

"Benefits and Costs of the Clean Air Act 1990–2020." U.S. EPA. https://www.epa.gov/clean-air-act-overview/benefits-and-costs-clean-air-act-1990-2020-second-prospective-study

"Cardiovascular Disease Deaths Reduced by Lead Service Line Replacement." Environmental Defense Fund. https://blogs.edf.org/health/2020/02/20/lslr-reduced-cardiovascular-disease-deaths/

"Catastrophic Out-of-Pocket Health Costs." Commonwealth Fund. https://www.commonwealthfund.org/publications/issue-briefs/2020/apr/catastrophic-out-of-pocket-costs-problem-middle-income

"Centi-Millionaire Report 2024." Henley Global. https://www.henleyglobal.com/publications/centi-millionaire-report-2024

"Costs of Inaction: Burden of Health." NRDC. https://www.nrdc.org/sites/default/files/costs-inaction-burden-health-report.pdf

"Economic Effects of a Federal Paid Family and Medical Leave Program." Congressional Budget Office. https://www.cbo.gov/publication/57631

"Effect of Operating Conditions and Technology on Residential Wood Stove Emissions of Criteria, Greenhouse Gas, and Hazardous Air Pollutants." Journal of the Air & Waste Management Association, 2025. https://www.tandfonline.com/doi/full/10.1080/10962247.2025.2488807#abstract

"EPA Announces $3 Billion for Lead in Drinking Water." U.S. EPA. https://www.epa.gov/newsreleases/epa-announces-3-billion-new-funding-states-reduce-lead-drinking-water

"Estimating health and economic benefits of reductions in air pollution from agriculture." Science of the Total Environment, 2017. https://www.sciencedirect.com/science/article/abs/pii/S0048969717334836

"Exporting Used Textiles Helps Global and Local Economies." USDA. https://www.usda.gov/about-usda/news/blog/exporting-used-textiles-helps-global-and-local-economies

"Global Tuberculosis Report 2023." World Health Organization. https://www.who.int/teams/global-programme-on-tuberculosis-and-lung-health/tb-reports/global-tuberculosis-report-2023/financing-for-tb-prevention--diagnostic-and-treatment-services

"How Much Would High-Quality Universal Early Care Cost?" Education Week. https://www.edweek.org/teaching-learning/how-much-would-high-quality-universal-early-care-cost-try-140-billion-a-year/2018/03

"Identifying Sources of Deadly Air Pollution in the U.S." Stanford Sustainability. https://sustainability.stanford.edu/news/identifying-sources-deadly-air-pollution-us

"Implementing Wood-Burning Changeout Campaigns." U.S. EPA. https://www.epa.gov/burnwise/implementing-wood-burning-change out-campaigns-and-examples-programs

"Inside Wealth." CNBC Newsletter, March 6, 2025. https://link.cnbc.com/public/38877848

"Key Findings: State of the Air." American Lung Association. https://www.lung.org/research/sota/key-findings

"Mayors' Roadmap: Paving the Way for Healthier Cities." Environmental Defense Fund. https://www.edf.org/media/mayors-roadmap-paving-way-healthier-cities

"Medical Bankruptcy: Still Common Despite the Affordable Care Act." American Journal of Public Health, 2019. https://pmc.ncbi.nlm.nih.gov/articles/PMC6366487/

"National Health Expenditure Data." Centers for Medicare & Medicaid Services. https://www.cms.gov/data-research/statistics-trends-and-reports/national-health-expenditure-data/nhe-fact-sheet

"Reducing Mortality from Air Pollution in the United States by

Targeting Specific Emission Sources." Environmental Science & Technology Letters, 2020. https://pubs.acs.org/doi/10.1021/acs.estlett.0c00424

"The Diaper Need Overview." National Diaper Bank Network. https://nationaldiaperbanknetwork.org/wp-content/uploads/2022/12/NDBN_DiaperNeed_Overview_Dec_2022-.pdf

"The Global Fund Investment Case." The Global Fund. http://theglobalfund.org/en/investment-case/

"The Knight Frank Wealth Report." Knight Frank. https://www.knightfrank.com/wealthreport

"UNFPA report links falling birth rates to cost of living, sexist norms, fear of the future." United Nations Population Fund. https://www.unfpa.org/press/unfpa-report-links-falling-birth-rates-cost-living-sexist-norms-fear-future

"What Babies Really Cost." What to Expect. https://www.whattoexpect.com/getting-pregnant/preparing-for-baby/work-and-finance/what-babies-really-cost.aspx

"What Really Happens to Unwanted Clothes." Green America. https://greenamerica.org/unraveling-fashion-industry/what-really-happens-unwanted-clothes

"What Would It Cost to Replace All the Nation's Lead Water Pipes?" Brookings Institution. https://www.brookings.edu/articles/what-would-it-cost-to-replace-all-the-nations-lead-water-pipes/

"What would it take to end extreme poverty? | Paul Niehaus | TEDxBoston." https://www.youtube.com/watch?v=vrQwahPQ6YI

"Wood-Burning Stove Installation Cost." Angi. https://www.angi.com/articles/wood-burning-stove-installation-cost.htm

"Wood-Burning Stove Installation Cost." EPA Fast Facts, 2016. https://www.epa.gov/sites/default/files/2016-11/documents/kit_2_fast_facts.pdf

Chapter 6

"Corporate Tax Rates by Country 2024." Tax Foundation. https://taxfoundation.org/data/all/global/corporate-tax-rates-by-country-2024/

"Diabetes Interventions." CDC. https://www.cdc.gov/nccdphp/priorities/diabetes-interventions.html

"High Fructose Corn Syrup." EBSCO Research Starters. https://www.ebsco.com/research-starters/nutrition-and-dietetics/high-fructose-corn-syrup-hfcs

"Obesity and Agricultural Subsidies." Mount Sinai. https://www.mountsinai.org/files/ISMMS/Assets/Media/Profiles/MS_OpEd%20Ad_Obesity_final.pdf

"Top Commodities Receiving Subsidies 2024." Southwest Ledger. https://www.southwestledger.news/news/top-commodities-receiving-subsidies-2024

"We Subsidize Crops We Should Eat Less Of." NPR. https://www.npr.org/sections/thesalt/2016/07/18/486051480/we-subsidize-crops-we-should-eat-less-of-does-this-fatten-us-up

Chapter 7

"PLOS ONE study on charitable giving." PLOS.org. https://journals.plos.org/plosone/article?id=10.1371/journal.pone.0133193

Chapter 8

"Caring is Costly." Journal of Experimental Psychology: General. https://www.ovid.com/journals/jepge/abstract/10.1037/xge0001073~caring-is-costly-people-avoid-the-cognitive-work-of

"Global immunization efforts have saved at least 154 million lives over the past 50 years." UNICEF. https://www.unicef.org/lac/en/press-releases/global-immunization-efforts-saved-154-million-lives-over-past-50-years

"Our Epidemic of Loneliness and Isolation." Department of Health & Human Services. https://www.hhs.gov/sites/default/files/surgeon-general-social-connection-advisory.pdf

"Tainted Altruism: When Doing Some Good Is Evaluated as Worse Than Doing No Good at All." Psychological Science. https://journals.sagepub.com/doi/abs/10.1177/0956797613504785

"The many benefits of giving: Prosocial spending and happiness." Current Directions in Psychological Science. https://www.evidence

basedmentoring.org/the-benefits-to-the-brain-of-charitable-giving-prosocial-spending-and-happiness

Chapter 9

"Forbes 39th Annual World's Billionaires List." Forbes. https://www.forbes.com/sites/chasewithorn/2025/04/01/forbes-39th-annual-worlds-billionaires-list-more-than-3000-worth-16-trillion/

Chapter 12

"Annual Report of General Motors Corporation 1951." HathiTrust Digital Library. https://babel.hathitrust.org/cgi/pt?id=osu.32435027473941&seq=29

APPENDIX B: MY NUMBER

Considerations and assumptions

To calculate my Number, I started by imagining my ideal lifestyle and estimating what it would cost. Next, I created four buckets of assets (stocks, private equity, real estate, other assets) and assigned a reasonable annual return for each. Finally, I calculated the total assets I would need to cover my lifestyle.

My largest asset will be my stock portfolio. Instead of holding cash, my portfolio will contain several million dollars in low-yielding Treasuries, which provide stability but reduce my annual return in most years. While I plan to hold some private equity investments, if I find that their returns don't justify their added effort and lower liquidity, I'll gradually rotate out of private equity and into stocks. I'm assuming my stock portfolio and private equity will both return 7.5% annually.

For real estate and "other assets" (cars, art, furniture, etc.), I'm assuming a 0% return. I currently own no income-generating real estate and have no plans to acquire any, so in that category I only have two homes: my primary residence and one vacation home. Because real estate generally appreciates in value, and because I'll gradually pay down my mortgages, I can expect the value of these assets to increase over time; in order to stick to my Number, I would offset these gains by selling more liquid assets (e.g. stocks) and donating the proceeds. As a high-income California resident, my effective tax rate is approximately 50%. I built in a 15% buffer to my Number as a hedge against future uncertainty.

One major difference between how I'm doing this exercise and how I imagine most wealthy people would do it is that I have not reached my Number (and may never reach it). This means I have to make assumptions about what my assets and lifestyle might look like, whereas someone who's already at or beyond their Number would know these things with certainty. Generally speaking, I would advise someone who hasn't reached their Number to do a ballpark calculation of it, and wait to do a detailed calculation until they're at or above their Number.

Assets

Here is a summary of my anticipated assets. This shows a $90 million net worth generating an annual pre-tax income of $5,925,000 and post-tax income of $2,962,500.

Asset	Value	Return (%)	Return ($)	% of assets
Stock Portfolio	$64,000,000	7.5%	$4,800,000	71%
Private Equity	$15,000,000	7.5%	$1,125,000	17%
Real Estate	$9,000,000	0%	$0	10%
Other Assets	$2,000,000	0%	$0	2%
Total	**$90,000,000**		**$5,925,000**	**100%**
Post-tax Income			***$2,962,500***	

Here is the detail on my real estate. I'm assuming a 50/50 debt-to-equity ratio, a 6.0% mortgage rate, annual insurance and maintenance costs equal to 1.5% of each home's value, and property tax of 1.2%. Mortgage, insurance, maintenance, and property tax expenses are in the next section.

Asset	**Value**	**Equity Value**	**Mortgage**
Primary Home	$10,000,000	$5,000,000	$5,000,000
Second Home	$8,000,000	$4,000,000	$4,000,000
Total Real Estate	$18,000,000	**$9,000,000**	$9,000,000

Lifestyle Cost

Here is a summary of my anticipated lifestyle cost. This is much higher than my current lifestyle cost, but again, the point of this exercise is to figure out the most comfortable lifestyle I would realistically want to live. If my actual lifestyle cost is less than this in any given year, I would simply donate the difference in order to maintain my Number.

Expense Item	**Monthly**	**Annual**
Homes		
Mortgages	$53,960	$647,520
Insurance and Maintenance	$22,500	$270,000
Property Tax	$18,000	$216,000
Travel		
Commercial Airfare	$9,000	$108,000
Private Charters	$9,000	$108,000
Accommodation	$8,000	$96,000
Activities	$7,000	$84,000
Hobbies		
Aviation	$8,000	$96,000
Sailing	$5,000	$60,000
Skiing	$3,000	$36,000
Golf	$1,000	$12,000
Other	$1,000	$12,000
Entertainment		
Parties and Social Events	$7,500	$90,000
Concerts, Plays, Comedy, etc.	$5,000	$60,000
Subscriptions, Memberships, Movies, etc.	$2,500	$30,000
Living Expenses		
School Tuition and Other Education	$15,000	$180,000
Kids (Clothes, Entertainment, Hobbies, etc.)	$8,000	$96,000
Groceries	$5,000	$60,000
Restaurants	$5,000	$60,000
Vehicles	$4,000	$48,000
Health and Pet Insurance	$4,000	$48,000
Shopping	$3,000	$36,000
Wellness	$3,000	$36,000
Professional Services	$3,000	$36,000
Utilities	$2,000	$24,000
Other Living Expenses	$2,000	$24,000
Total Lifestyle Cost	**$214,460**	**$2,573,520**

Here is the calculation for the annual income I would need to pay for my lifestyle. As you can see, my total pre-tax lifestyle cost is approximately equal to the pre-tax income ($5,925,000) generated by my assets. Given my 15% buffer, I can expect to donate about $400,000 per year to charity in order to maintain my Number.

Post-tax lifestyle cost	$2,573,520
+ Buffer (15%)	$386,028
= Total post-tax lifestyle cost	$2,959,548
+ Annual tax expense	$2,959,548
= Total pre-tax lifestyle cost	**$5,919,096**

APPENDIX C: $270 BILLION PER YEAR FOR HOUSING

This proposal came from the following Google Gemini prompt: "How would you allocate a $1 trillion annual budget to solve America's most pressing problems?" It came back with a $270 billion budget to address housing, which is detailed below. This is meant to get a conversation started, not as a bulletproof policy proposal, and should be taken as such.

I. Supply Initiatives – $145 billion

Proposal	Cost	Rationale
Affordable Housing Production Fund	$80B	The NLIHC estimates that the U.S. has a shortage of 7.3 million rental homes affordable to extremely low-income renters. To bridge this gap over a 10-year period, they advocate for a massive expansion of the National Housing Trust Fund (HTF).
Zoning Reform & Infrastructure Incentives	$35B	Exclusionary zoning (banning apartments/ duplexes) is the primary driver of high costs in high-opportunity areas. This fund would essentially pay cities to upgrade infrastructure (sewers, transit) in exchange for legalizing density.
Innovation & Cost Reduction	$15B	Construction costs have risen faster than inflation due to labor shortages and material costs. This fund targets "off-site construction" (modular housing) and R&D.
Landlord Tax Incentives for Affordability	$15B	Many landlords refuse vouchers due to administrative burdens or perceived risk. This fund pays small landlords to keep rents below market rate, helping middle class renters who don't qualify for vouchers but can't afford market prices.

Supporting Links

- Affordable Housing Production Fund
  - https://nlihc.org/housed
  - https://archives.hud.gov/news/2024/pr24-205.cfm
- Zoning Reform & Infrastructure Initiatives
  - https://www.brookings.edu/policy2020/bigideas/to-improve-housing-affordability-we-need-better-align

ment-of-zoning-taxes-and-subsidies/

- Innovation & Cost Reduction
  - https://ternercenter.berkeley.edu/research-and-policy/the-cost-of-building-housing-series/
  - https://www.huduser.gov/portal/portal/sites/default/files/pdf/Offsite-Construction-for-Housing-Research-Roadmap.pdf
- Landlord Tax Incentives for Affordability
  - https://www.urban.org/research/publication/pilot-study-landlord-acceptance-housing-choice-vouchers

II. Demand & Stability – $90 billion

Proposal	Cost	Rationale
Universal Housing Vouchers	$70B	Currently, only 1 in 4 eligible households receives rental assistance due to funding caps. This budget would cover the cost of guaranteeing vouchers to everyone who qualifies.
Permanent Supportive Housing	$20B	The US has about 600,000 people experiencing homelessness on any given night, and 120,000 chronically homeless people. This budget would fund a "surge" to build the necessary units and fund the social workers and medical staff needed to keep people housed.

Supporting Links

- Universal Housing Vouchers
  - http://cbpp.org/blog/expanding-housing-vouchers-would-cut-poverty-and-reduce-racial-disparities
- Permanent Supportive Housing
  - https://endhomelessness.org/state-of-homelessness/
  - https://www.csh.org/

    - https://www.congress.gov/bill/119th-congress/house-bill/4872

III. Ownership Initiatives – $35 billion

Proposal	Cost	Rationale
First-Time Down Payment Assistance	$35B	This fund would provide $25,000 to 1.4 million people per year to assist with a down payment on a home.

Supporting Links

- First-Time Down Payment Assistance
    - https://www.congress.gov/bill/119th-congress/house-bill/4069

ABOUT THE AUTHOR

Chris Kelly is a writer and entrepreneur living in San Francisco, California. *A Solution to Wealth Inequality* is his second book and first work of nonfiction.

wealthinequality.substack.com

www.ingramcontent.com/pod-product-compliance
Lightning Source LLC
LaVergne TN
LVHW101613210926
848480LV00008B/529

9798988263333